# WALKS
## IN
# CORSICA

Titles in the Footpaths of Europe Series

The publishers thank H. Viaux for permission to use his photographs in this book.

# WALKS
# IN
# CORSICA

Translated by Harry Pretty and Helen McPhail

Robertson McCarta

The publishers thank the following people for their help with this book: Isabelle
Daguin, Philippe Lambert, Serge Sineux, Harry Pretty, Daphne Terry.

First published in 1990 by

**Robertson McCarta Limited**
122 King's Cross Road
London WC1X 9DS

in association with

**Fédération Française de la Randonnée Pédestre**
8 Avenue Marceau
75008 Paris

**Managing Editor** Folly Marland
**Series designed** by Prue Bucknall
**Production** by Grahame Griffiths
**Typeset** by The Robertson Group, Llandudno
**Planning Map** by Rodney Paull

Printed and bound in Spain by Graficas Estella S.A.

British Library Cataloguing in Publication Data

Walks in Corsica. — (Footpaths of Europe).
    1. France. Corsica — Visitors' guides
    I. Series
    914.4'94504838

    ISBN 1-85365-199-0

# CONTENTS

*The walks and maps*

## Walk 1      23

*GR20*    Calenzana ► Carrefour de Sentiers ► Refuge de Carozzu ►
Haut Asco ► Bergeries de Ballone ► Calasima ► Refuge de Manganu
► Refuge de Pietra Piana ► Refuge de l'Onda ► Bocca Palmente ►
Refuge de Capanelle ► Col de Verde ► Refuge D'Usciolu ► Col de
Bavella ► **Conca**

## Walk 2      65

*TMEM*    Calenzana ► Bonifatu ► Tuvarelli ► Galeria ► Girolata
Serriera ► Evisa ► **Cargese**

## Walk 3      85

Sermano ► Corte ► Calacuccia ► Albertacce ► Evisa ► Marignana
► Revinda/E Case ► **Cargese**
Alternative route Sermano to Marignana:
Sermano ► Canaglia (Vivario) ► Pastricciola ► Soccia ► **Marignana**

## Walk 4      99

Ghisonaccia ► Serra-di-Fiumorbu ► Cozzano ► Tasso ► Guitera-les-
Bains ► Quasquara ► Col Saint Georges ► **Ajaccio**
Alternative route: Cozzano ► Zicavo ► **Guitera-les-Bains**

## Walk 5      111

Porto Vecchio ► Levie ► Bavella ► Zonza ► Quenza ► Serra-di-
Scopamene ► Sainte-Lucie-de-Tallano ► Loreto di Tallano ► Fozzano
► **Propriano**
Alternative route: Loreto di Tallano ► Burgo ► **Propriano**

# Key to IGN Maps

Motorway, dual carriageway _____

Major road, four lanes or more _____

Main road, two-lane or three-lane, wide _____

Main road, two-lane, narrow _____

Narrow road, regularly surfaced _____

Other narrow road: regularly surfaced; irregularly surfaced _____

Field track, forest track, felling track, footpath _____

Track of disused road. Road under construction _____

Road through embankment, cutting. Tree-lined road or track _____

Bank. Hedge, line of trees _____

Railway: double track, single track. Electrified line. Station, waiting line. Halt, stop _____

Sidings or access lines. Narrow gauge line. Rack railway _____

Electricity transmission line. Cable railway. Ski lift _____

National boundary with markers _____

Boundary and administrative centre of department, district _____

Boundary and administrative centre of canton, commune _____

Boundary of military camp, firing range _____

Boundary of State forest, National Park, outer zone of National Park _____

Triangulation points _____

Church, chapel, shrine. Cross, tomb, religious statue. Cemetery _____

Watch tower, fortress. Windmill, wind-pump. Chimney _____

Storage tank: oil, gas. Blast furnace. Pylon. Quarry _____

Cave. Monument, pillar. Castle. Ruins _____

Megalithic monument: dolmen, menhir. Viewpoint. Campsite _____

Market-hall, shed, glasshouse, casemate _____

Access to underground workings. Refuge. Ski-jump _____

Population/thousands _____

Bridge. Footbridge. Ford. Ferry _____

Lake, pool. Area liable to flooding. Marsh _____

Source, spring. Well, water-tank. Water-tower, reservoir _____

Watercourse lined with trees. Waterfall. Dam. Dyke _____

Navigable canal, feeder or irrigator. Lock, machine-operated. Underground channel.

Contour lines. 10 m. interval. Hollow. Small basin. Scree _____

Principal / Secondary

Possibly private or controlled access

For shooting times, go to town hall or gendarmerie

**PF** ... **SP**

**CT** ... **C**

**Tr** — **Chem.**

**Mon.** — **P.V.**

**Mine** — **Cave**

183,2    0,4    0,15    0,06

Ch⁰ᵛ d'Eau

| Woodland | Scrub | Orchard, plantation | Vines | Ricefield |

All maps are IGN Orange series. 1:50 000    © I.G.N. – Paris

6

# A note from the publisher

The books in this French Walking Guide series are produced in association and with the help of the Fédération Française de la Randonnée Pédestre (French ramblers' association) — generally known as the FFRP.

The FFRP is a federal organisation and is made up of regional, local and many other associations and bodies that form its constituent parts. Individual membership is through these various local organisations. The FFRP therefore acts as an umbrella organisation overseeing the waymarking of footpaths, training and the publishing of the Topoguides, detailed guides to the Grande Randonnée footpaths.

There are at present about 170 Topoguides in print, compiled and written by local members of the FFRP, who are responsible for waymarking the walks — so they are well researched and accurate.

We have translated the main itinerary descriptions, amalgamating and adapting several Topoguides to create new regional guides. We have retained the basic Topoguide structure, indicating length and times of walks, and the Institut Géographique National (official French survey) maps overlaid with the routes.

The information contained in this guide is the latest available at the time of going to print. However, as publishers we are aware that this kind of information is continually changing and we are anxious to enhance and improve the guides as much as possible. We encourage you to send us suggestions, criticisms and those little bits of information you may wish to share with your fellow walkers. Our address is: Robertson McCarta, 122 King's Cross Road, London WC1X 9DS.

We shall be happy to offer a free copy of any one of these books to any reader whose suggestions are subsequently incorporated into a new edition.

It is possible to create a variety of routes by referring to the walks in the contents page and to the planning map (inside the front cover). Transport is listed in the alphabetical index in the back of the book and there is an accommodation guide.

# KEY

**Gournay**

This example shows that you can expect the walk from Gournay to Arbois to take 2 hours, 10 minutes.

2:10

**ARBOIS**
🏠 🏠 ✕ 🏪 🚌
*14th century church*

Arbois has a variety of facilities, including hotels and buses. Hotel addresses and bus/train connections may be listed in the index at the back of the book.

A grey arrow indicates an alternative route that leaves and returns to the main route.

**Detour**

indicates a short detour off the route to a town with facilities or to an interesting sight.

---

**Symbols:**

🏠 hotel;

⌂ youth hostel, hut or refuge;

🅰 camping;

✕ restaurant;

🍷 cafe;

🏪 shops;

🚉 railway station;

🚌 buses;

⛴ ferry;

ℹ tourist information;

# THE FOOTPATHS OF FRANCE

## by Robin Neillands

**W**hy should you go walking in France? Well, walking is fun and as for France, Danton summed up the attractions of that country with one telling phrase: 'Every man has two countries,' he said, 'his own . . . and France.' That is certainly true in my case and I therefore consider it both a pleasure and an honour to write this general introduction to these footpath guides to France. A pleasure because walking in or through France is my favourite pastime, an honour because these excellent English language guides follow in the course set by those Topo-guides published in French by the Fédération Française pour la Randonnée Pédestre, which set a benchmark for quality that all footpath guides might follow. Besides, I believe that good things should be shared and walking in France is one of the most pleasant activities I know.

I have been walking in France for over thirty years. I began by rambling — or rather ambling — through the foothills of the Pyrenees, crossing over into Spain past the old Hospice de France, coming back over the Somport Pass in a howling blizzard, which may account for the fact that I totally missed two sets of frontier guards on both occasions. Since then I have walked in many parts of France and even from one end of it to the other, from the Channel to the Camargue, and I hope to go on walking there for many years to come.

The attractions of France are legion, but there is no finer way to see and enjoy them than on foot. France has two coasts, at least three mountain ranges — the Alps, Pyrenees and the Massif Central — an agreeable climate, a great sense of space, good food, fine wines and, believe it or not, a friendly and hospitable people. If you don't believe me, go there on foot and see for yourself. Walking in France will appeal to every kind of walker, from the day rambler to the backpacker, because above all, and in the nicest possible way, the walking in France is well organised, but those Francophiles who already know France well will find it even more pleasurable if they explore their favourite country on foot.

### The GR system

The Grande Randonnée (GR) footpath network now consists of more than 40,000 kilometres (25,000 miles) of long-distance footpath, stretching into every part of France, forming a great central sweep around Paris, probing deeply into the Alps, the Pyrenees, and the volcanic cones of the Massif Central. This network, the finest system of footpaths in Europe, is the creation of that marvellously named organisation, *la Fédération Française de Randonnée Pédestre, Comité National des Sentiers de Grande Randonnée,* which I shall abbreviate to FFRP-CNSGR. Founded in 1948, and declaring that, *'un jour de marche, huit jours de santé* the FFRP-CNSGR has flourished for four decades and put up the now familiar red-and -white waymarks in every corner of the country. Some of these footpaths are classic walks, like the famous GR65, *Le Chemin de St. Jacques,* the ancient Pilgrim Road to Compostela, the TMB, the *Tour du Mont Blanc,* which circles the mountain through France,

Switzerland and Italy, or the 600-mile long GR3, the *Sentier de la Loire,* which runs from the Ardèche to the Atlantic, to give three examples from the hundred or so GR trails available. In addition there is an abundance of GR du Pays or regional footpaths, like the *Sentier de la Haute Auvergne,* and the *Sentier Tour des Monts d'Aubrac.* A 'Tour' incidentally, is usually a circular walk. Many of these regional or provincial GR trails are charted and waymarked in red-and-yellow by local outdoor organisations such as ABRI (Association Bretonne des Relais et Itineraires) for Brittany, or CHAMINA for the Massif Central. The walker in France will soon become familiar with all these footpath networks, national, regional or local, and find them the perfect way into the heart and heartland of France. As a little bonus, the GR networks are expanding all the time, with the detours — or *varientes* — off the main route eventually linking with other GR paths or *varientes* and becoming GR trails in their own right.

Walkers will find the GR trails generally well marked and easy to follow, and they have two advantages over the footpaths commonly encountered in the UK. First, since they are laid out by local people, they are based on intricate local knowledge of the local sights. If there is a fine view, a mighty castle or a pretty village on your footpath route, your footpath through France will surely lead you to it. Secondly, all French footpaths are usually well provided with a wide range of comfortable country accommodation, and you will discover that the local people, even the farmers, are well used to walkers and greet them with a smile, a *'Bonjour'* and a *'bonne route'.*

**Terrain and Climate**

As a glance at these guides or any Topo-guide will indicate, France has a great variety of terrain. France is twice the size of the UK and many natural features are also on a larger scale. There are three main ranges of mountains, the Alps contain the highest mountain in Europe, the Pyrenees go up to 10,000 ft, the Massif Central peaks to over 6000 ft, and there are many similar ranges with hills which overtop our highest British peak, Ben Nevis. On the other hand, the Auvergne and the Jura have marvellous open ridge walking, the Cévennes are steep and rugged, the Ardeche and parts of Provence are hot and wild, the Île de France, Normandy, Brittany and much of Western France is green and pleasant, not given to extremes. There is walking in France for every kind of walker, but given such a choice the wise walker will consider the complications of terrain and weather before setting out, and go suitably equipped.

France enjoys three types of climate: continental, oceanic, and mediterranean. South of the Loire it will certainly be hot to very hot from mid-April to late September. Snow can fall on the mountains above 4000 ft from mid-October and last until May, or even lie year-round on the tops and in couloirs; in the high hills an ice-axe is never a frill. I have used one by the Brêche de Roland in the Pyrenees in mid-June.

Wise walkers should study weather maps and forecasts carefully in the week before they leave for France, but can generally expect good weather from May to October, and a wide variety of weather — the severity depending on the terrain — from mid-October to late Spring.

**Accommodation**

The walker in France can choose from a wide variety of accommodation with the asurance that the walker will always be welcome. This can range from country hotels to wild mountain pitches, but to stay in comfort, many walkers will travel light and overnight in the comfortable hotels of the *Logis de France* network.

**Logis de France:** The *Logis de France* is a nationwide network of small, family-run country hotels, offering comfortable accommodation and excellent food. *Logis* hotels are graded and can vary from a simple, one-star establishment, with showers and linoleum, to a four- or five-star *logis* with gastronomic menus and deep pile-carpets. All offer excellent value for money, and since there are over 5,000 scattered across the French countryside, they provide a good focus for a walking day. An annual guide to the *Logis* is available from the French Government Tourist Office, 178 Piccadilly, London W1V 0AL, Tel (01) 491 7622.

**Gîtes d'étape:** A *gîte d'étape* is best imagined as an unmanned youth hostel for outdoor folk of all ages. They lie along the footpath networks and are usually signposted or listed in the guides. They can be very comfortable, with bunk beds, showers, a well equipped kitchen, and in some cases they have a warden, a *guardien*, who may offer meals. *Gîtes d'étape* are designed exclusively for walkers, climbers, cyclists, cross country skiers or horse-riders. A typical price (1990) would be Fr.25 for one night. *Gîtes d'étape* should not be confused with a *Gîte de France*. A *gîte* — usually signposted as *'Gîte de France'* — is a country cottage available for a holiday let, though here too, the owner may be more than willing to rent it out as overnight accommodation.

**Youth hostels:** Curiously enough, there are very few Youth Hostels in France outside the main towns. A full list of the 200 or so available can be obtained from the Youth Hostel Association (YHA), Trevelyan House, St. Albans, Herts AL1 2DY.

**Pensions or cafes:** In the absence of an hotel, a *gîte d'étape* or a youth hostel, all is not lost. France has plenty of accommodation and an enquiry at the village cafe or bar will usually produce a room. The cafe/hotel may have rooms or suggest a nearby pension or a *chambre d'hôte*. Prices start at around Fr.50 for a room, rising to say, Fr.120. (1990 estimate).

**Chambres d'hôte:** A *chambre d'hôte* is a guest room, or, in English terms, a bed-and-breakfast, usually in a private house. Prices range from about Fr.60 a night. *Chambres d'hôte* signs are now proliferating in the small villages of France and especially if you can speak a little French are an excellent way to meet the local people. Prices (1990) are from, say, Fr.70 for a room, not per person.

**Abris:** *Abris,* shelters or mountain huts can be found in the mountain regions, where they are often run by the *Club Alpin Francais,* an association for climbers. They range from the comfortable to the primitive, are often crowded and are sometimes reserved for members. Details from the Club Alpin Francais, 7 Rue la Boétie, Paris 75008, France.

**Camping:** French camp sites are graded from one to five star, but are generally very good at every level, although the facilities naturally vary from one cold tap to shops, bars and heated pools. Walkers should not be deterred by the *'Complet'* (Full) sign on the gate or office window: a walker's small tent will usually fit in somewhere. *Camping à la ferme,* or farm camping, is increasingly popular, more primitive — or less regimented — than the official sites, but widely available and perfectly adequate. Wild camping is officially not permitted in National Parks, but unofficially if you are over 1,500m away from a road, one hour's walk from a *gîte* or campsite, and where possible ask permission, you should have no trouble. French country people will always assist the walker to find a pitch.

## The law for walkers

The country people of France seem a good deal less concerned about their 'rights' than the average English farmer or landowner. I have never been ordered off land in France or greeted with anything other than friendliness . . . maybe I've been lucky. As a rule, walkers in France are free to roam over all open paths and tracks. No decent walker will leave gates open, trample crops or break down walls, and taking fruit from gardens or orchards is simply stealing. In some parts of France there are local laws about taking chestnuts, mushrooms (and snails), because these are cash crops. Signs like *Réserve de Chasse*, or *Chasse Privé* indicate that the shooting is reserved for the landowner. As a general rule, behave sensibly and you will be tolerated everywhere, even on private land.

## The country code

Walkers in France should obey the *Code du Randonneur.*

- Love and respect nature.
- Avoid unnecessary noise.
- Destroy nothing.
- Do not leave litter.
- Do not pick flowers or plants.
- Do not disturb wildlife.
- Re-close all gates.
- Protect and preserve the habitat.
- No smoking or fires in the forests. (This rule is essential and is actively enforced by foresters and police).
- Respect and understand the country way of life and the country people.
- Think of others as you think of yourself.

## Transport

Transportation to and within France is generally excellent. There are no less than nine Channel ports: Dunkirk, Calais, Boulogne, Dieppe, Le Havre, Caen/Ouistreham, Cherbourg, Saint-Malo and Roscoff, and a surprising number of airports served by direct flights from the UK. Although some of the services are seasonal, it is often possible to fly direct to Toulouse, Poitiers, Nantes, Perpignan, Montpellier, indeed to many provincial cities, as well as Paris and such obvious destinations as Lyon and Nice. Within France the national railway, the SNCF, still retains a nationwide network. Information, tickets and a map can be obtained from the SNCF. France also has a good country bus service and the *gare routière* is often placed just beside the railway station. Be aware though, that many French bus services only operate within the *département,* and they do not generally operate from one provincial city to the next. I cannot encourage people to hitch-hike, which is both illegal and risky, but walkers might consider a taxi for their luggage. Almost every French village has a taxi driver who will happily transport your rucksacks to the next night-stop, fifteen to twenty miles away, for Fr.50 a head or even less.

## Money

Walking in France is cheap, but banks are not common in the smaller villages, so carry a certain amount of French money and the rest in traveller's cheques or Eurocheques, which are accepted everywhere.

## Clothing and equipment

The amount of clothing and equipment you will need depends on the terrain, the length of the walk, the time of your visit, the accommodation used. Outside the mountain areas it is not necessary to take the full range of camping or backpacking gear. I once walked across France from the Channel to the Camargue along the Grande Randonneé footpaths in March, April and early May and never needed to use any of the camping gear I carried in my rucksack because I found hotels everywhere, even in quite small villages.

Essential items are:

**In summer:** light boots, a hat, shorts, suncream, lip salve, mosquito repellent, sunglasses, a sweater, a windproof cagoule, a small first-aid kit, a walking stick.
**In winter:** a change of clothing, stormproof outer garments, gaiters, hat, lip salve, a companion.
**In the mountains at any time:** large-scale maps (1:25,000), a compass, an ice-axe. In winter, add a companion and ten-point crampons.
**At any time:** a phrase book, suitable maps, a dictionary, a sense of humour.

The best guide to what to take lies in the likely weather and the terrain. France tends to be informal, so there is no need to carry a jacket or something smart for the evenings. I swear by Rohan clothing, which is light, smart and functional. The three things I would never go without are light, well-broken-in boots and several pairs of loop-stitched socks, and my walking stick.

## Health hazards:

Health hazards are few. France can be hot in summer, so take a full water-bottle and refill at every opportunity. A small first-aid kit is sensible, with plasters and 'mole-skin' for blisters, but since prevention is better than the cure, loop-stitched socks and flexible boots are better. Any French chemist — a *pharmacie* — is obliged to render first-aid treatment for a small fee. These pharmacies can be found in most villages and large towns and are marked by a green cross.

Dogs are both a nuisance and a hazard. All walkers in France should carry a walking stick to fend off aggressive curs. Rabies — *la rage* — is endemic and anyone bitten must seek immediate medical advice. France also possesses two types of viper, which are common in the hill areas of the south. In fairness, although I found my walking stick indispensable, I must add that in thirty years I have never even seen a snake or a rabid dog. In case of real difficulty, dial 17 for the police and the ambulance.

## Food and wine

One of the great advantages with walking in France is that you can end the day with a good meal and not gain an ounce. French country cooking is generally excellent and good value for money, with the price of a four-course menu starting at about Fr.45. The ingredients for the mid-day picnic can be purchased from the village shops and these also sell wine. Camping-Gaz cylinders and cartridges are widely available, as is 2-star petrol for stoves. Avoid naked fires.

## Preparation
The secret of a good walk lies in making adequate preparations before you set out. It pays to be fit enough to do the daily distance at the start. Much of the necessary information is contained in this guide, but if you need more, look in guidebooks or outdoor magazines, or ask friends.

## The French
I cannot close this introduction without saying a few words about the French, not least because the walker in France is going to meet rather more French people than, say, a motorist will, and may even meet French people who have never met a foreigner before. It does help if the visitor speaks a little French, even if only to say 'bonjour' and 'Merci' and 'S'il vous plait'. The French tend to be formal so it pays to be polite, to say 'hello', to shake hands. I am well aware that relations between France and England have not always been cordial over the last six hundred years or so, but I have never met with hostility of any kind in thirty years of walking through France. Indeed, I have always found that if the visitor is prepared to meet the French halfway, they will come more than halfway to greet him or her in return, and are both friendly and hospitable to the passing stranger.

As a final tip, try smiling. Even in France, or especially in France, a smile and a 'pouvez vous m'aider?' (Can you help me?) will work wonders. That's my last bit of advice, and all I need do now is wish you 'Bonne Route' and good walking in France.

# WALKS IN CORSICA

## by Harry Pretty

Among those interested in long-distance mountain walking Corsica has for some time been identified with the GR20, and several articles in various journals, particularly during the last 8 years, have considerably increased the number of British participants. The route has justifiably developed a reputation as one of the most technically difficult of all European GRs. But such judgements are subjective and relative only to personal experience. Nevertheless the GR20 is unique in one respect: it provides a high-level walk for almost the entire length of a singularly beautiful island. It is relatively short but in its achievement one senses having made a journey in classical style. Like all such journeys, and regardless of direction north or south, it unfolds in a series of subtle passages interspersed with sustained periods of high drama - a complete reflection of the island's character.

### The Island and its People

The mountain configuration in Corsica is basically simple. A high watershed ridge runs from north to south, rather like an open letter `S', with long ridge spurs branching off both sides on approximately northeast and southwest axes. The main ridge generally diminishes in height southwards so that most of the highest peaks and passes are in the north, but several isolated summits in the southern half are over 2,100 metres.

This mountain structure creating a continuous high barrier between east and west, with equally high transverse ridges separating deeply cut basins on either side of the main divide, has had a profound effect on the life of the Corsican people. To understand the complex history of the island and its invaders, from the Graeco-Romans right down to and including French intervention, and the inspired rebellions towards a self-made democracy by Pasquale Paoli in the 18th century, one needs to recognize the regional characteristics of Corsican society, and the separate ways of indigenous life, imposed by these divisive mountain barricades.

Walking through Corsica, one encounters a landscape whose harshness seems in accord with the violence that has spun a convoluted thread down the years. To read Dorothy Carrington's unequalled portrait, `Granite Island', re-issued by Penguin, is to gain some insight and find significance in the landscape, beyond mere mountain shapes. The aura of the past can still be felt in the mountain villages, perched like birds' nests on the crags, in the monumental stone façades and black alleyways of Sartene, and in the simple stone bergeries that seem to grow from the earth in their sheltered hollows as organically as the enveloping maquis. At its most romantically spectacular past and present are fused in the sighting of a lone hunter, clad in black corduroys, great black wide brimmed hat rakishly askew, astride a splendid mountain pony as black as his clothes - with a volley of shots skywards just as likely a greeting as a further volley in farewell.

Only in the Greek Mani and in the highlands of Crete does one find any true parallel. It is probably no coincidence that the native populations of such places have retained their identities regardless of temporary overlords. They have retired to their towered villages or their mountain fastnesses, and maintained their mysterious fascination with death and the deadly obligation of the Vendetta. Their bandits d'honneur are men of recent history. But many people will walk through Corsica unmindful of its history, or travel from Calvi to Calenzana in an air conditioned taxi without a thought for the low line of hills west of the Citadel, where the British in 1794 started their siege, and Nelson, manning a shore-based battery, lost his right eye from an `explosion of stones'. But this is a matter of taste. The highlands of Corsica have enough to offer the modern walker simply in terms of their wild beauty, their flora and fauna, the serious nature of the terrain, and the challenging prospect of long, high-level distances without easy road access or the means of re-provisioning, except by making equally challenging detours.

## The GR20

A glance at the map is sufficient to indicate the basic simplicity of the GR20, and to show that in the entire length of the route only four roads crossing the main watershed are encountered. At 3 of these crossings - Vergio, Vizzavona, and Bavella - it is possible to take on further provisions. The fourth, Col de Verde, has only a small bar-restaurant, a private refuge, and no basic food on offer. Even the Hotel Castel de Verghio currently carries only a very limited amount of food for sale, so that if one intends to walk the entire route in the generally prescribed time of 15 days, the logistics of food supply, and decisions in terms of what weight to carry, are of vital importance. The refuges of the Parc Regionale are well spaced along the entire length of the route, but as they provide only shelter, food for several days must be carried at all times.

This guide is arranged, in the tradition of the FFRP Topoguide, following the GR20 north to south. Many people walk the route in the opposite direction and, as for all GRs, the red and white way marking is equally appropriate for both. In walking south there is a tendency for the sun to be en-face but in summer, the sun being high overhead for most of the day, this is of little significance. The choice is likely to be made more for reasons of topography and the particular section of the route to be traversed. The overall route is neatly divided into northern and southern sections by the very accessible road and railway intersection at Vizzavona and, since the northern part is generally considered the more scenically spectacular and physically demanding, many people choose to complete a section of the total distance according to their experience and/or time available.

The fact that Calvi, close to Calenzana in the north, is more directly accessible by air, sea and train than Porto Vecchio, its equivalent in the south, is also a strong influence. The Gîte d'étape at Calenzana makes a good base, and an ideal departure point for what is in essence a great adventure. Conca, as yet with only a private camp site, and accessible only from Sainte-Lucie by taxi (bus from Porto Vecchio or Bastia), demands a more positive choice as a starting point.

This description of the GR20 assumes a continuous flow-pattern from end to end and is not separated into defined stages. Walkers are left to plan their own walk according to their own levels of fitness, the weight of food carried, and time available. Detours to obtain food which may involve an additional day's walk, there and back to the GR, alternative points of access and egress, alternative routes between fixed points on the line of the GR, either to diminish or increase the level of difficulty, and other significant issues, such as the availability of water, are all referred to at the point at which they occur. Some of these are waymarked in yellow, unless otherwise indicated, as are the `high mountain' alternative routes suggested.

The times given between departure points are based on those advised in the FFRP Topoguide, which assumes that the entire route can be accomplished in 15 days. But such times are notoriously difficult to assess for the `average' person, and the GR20 can hardly be defined as a `walk' like the Pennine Way or any other British long-distance route. Much of it follows steep, rough paths, strewn with loose boulders, often badly eroded where the line does not follow an old well-graded shepherd's track. On extensive sections hands are required to maintain balance, and frequently one is rock scrambling along or below pinnacled ridges with considerable exposure. Consequently the speed of travel varies greatly between individuals. Today in mountain areas throughout Europe fit young men and women, lightly clad and in trainers, carrying nothing more than a day sack, can move fast over long distances relying on speed and fitness, unlike my generation of mountaineer-walkers who never feel entirely confident without the full complement of high mountain equipment, with bivvy bag, cooking stove, heavy leather boots etc. There is of course, the inevitable compromise but one should never, in any circumstances, underestimate the potential dangers of weather and natural terrain that are inherent in a long-distance `haute-route' of this quality.

### Subsidiary Walks `Between Sea and Mountain' and `From Sea to Sea'

Other long-distance walks opened up by the Corsican Regional Nature Park are included in this Guide, and there are a number of options from which to choose a route. Those not prepared for the stark challenge of walking the GR20 end to end can combine its various parts with one or other of the coast-to-coast itineraries, Walks 2-5 - though north of Col de Verghio this is not much of an option. Perhaps the most exciting aspect of the GR20 between Calenzana and the Col de Verghio is that it exists at all as a walking route for, without the dramatic linkage, across the Col de la Solitude, practicable only in good weather, this most dramatic area of Corsica would be closed to all but the mountaineer proper.

Walking the GR20 itself will not give much of an insight into the Corsican way of life; as a high-mountain walk it avoids the villages on either side, which are seen only from above or at a distance as clusters of reddish-pink roofs and grey stone set among dark forest. Vizzavona is the only place of permanent settlement between Calenzana and Conca, and as I have mentioned, detours or alternative routes must be taken to reach other habitations. However, the other long-distance walks described, which are waymarked in orange, are largely based on old mule tracks and the ancient routes of transhumance that cross the island connecting the villages with high summer pastures. They progress from village to village, crossing intermediate ridges, following forested valleys and, in some cases, crossing the main watershed ridge and the line of the GR20. They are well provided with refuges and alternative gîtes, and there is little need to carry a food supply since there is ample opportunity to buy provisions along the route.

### The Mountain Climate

Specific comparison illustrates the variations that can occur. In June 1980, after a heavy late snowfall in the European Alps, we encountered snow well below the level of the old D'Altoro Refuge, the Cirque de la Solitude required vigorous use of an ice axe. From 100 metres above the Manganu Refuge there was continuous snow down to the level of the Pietra-Piana Refuge and simultaneously the mountain streams were in a torrential condition and some not easy to cross. Conversely, in June 1989 snow was hardly visible except in sheltered northern hollows, streams were diminished, and the Ficarella stream had virtually dried up 3 kilometres below the Bocca Reza, Maison Forestière, where I had swum in deep, fast moving water in June 1983. It is therefore important to have some knowledge of the general weather patterns which, as in all high mountain areas, will have a profound influence on choice of season and appropriate clothing and equipment.

At coastal level, Corsica has a typical Mediterranean climate with prevailing west and north-westerly winds that frequently bring cloud. But these conditions vary with altitude and mountain form, and at all seasons, micro climatic conditions can produce widely different temperature, rainfall, and snow-cover on either side of the main divide and even in adjacent valleys. Usually the wettest months are March and April (following the `White Spring' of February), and October and November. Coastal rain falls as snow in the mountains and residual snow can lie on north and northeast facing slopes well into June, and occasionally throughout the year in isolated patches. In the mountains each year is different and has to be taken at face value.

There is a general consensus that the GR20 is open for normal passage from the first week of July to the end of October. Between the first week of June and mid-July conditions will vary, and ice-axes, with a 40 metre length of light climbing line per group, may be advisable, always subject to individual and collective experience. A well experienced party equipped with ice-axes, can make good times on good spring snow. But one such party encountered an avalanche at the end of May in the Cirque de la Solitude, where they were forced to bivvy until conditions improved.

Temperatures increase rapidly in July, August and into September and there is a consequential loss of water flow in mountain streams. Although temperatures are to some extent modified by increasing altitude, serious dehydration can occur on exposed high-altitude sections of the routes and, in the rainless months of high summer, streams will be mostly non-existent. All Park refuges have a good water supply, with the possible exception of Ciottulu di i Mori, but it is important to note alternative sources, particularly over critical sections of the walk. A water bottle is an essential piece of equipment for walking in Corsica.

Violent electrical storms are another summer phenomenon. Unsettled weather and turbulent skies normally provide enough warning, but, if in doubt assume the worst and stay away from high or even relatively low exposed areas. The storms can be extremely vicious, accompanied by ferocious localised winds with remarkable concentrations of electrical discharge. Electrical storms and forest fires are perhaps the greatest dangers to mountain walkers in Corsica.

**Terrain and Geology**
Generally these watershed ranges are volcanic in origin and consist of granites, granulites, rhyolites and a beautiful reddish porphyry. Many forms of conglomerate are also distributed throughout the main ranges and in this context one should mention the strange holes which in some places permeate the rock in the manner of Gruyère Cheese. Several of them referred to locally as `tafoni', penetrate the entire mountain mass, and have lent their name to the famous Capu Tafonatu in the north, and Punta Tafonatu di Paliri in the south.

Widespread glaciation and subsequent erosion have had a significant effect on the current topography, particularly among the highest summits in the north. The largest glaciers originally flowed to the east, and subsequent erosion has produced a striking asymmetry in the valleys which now drain east and west from the main divide, effectively pushing the watershed ridge further west and creating long, deep, gorge-like valleys on the east. Most of the highest peaks are still found to the east of the north-south watershed ridge. Glaciation has not played so significant a role in the south, where a profusion of aiguilles and saw toothed ridges rise abruptly from relatively low altitudes. Only in a few instances do these summits exceed 1,500 metres, well below the level of the areas affected by glaciation.

This brief reference to basic geology and its residual forms ignores the folded schists which comprise the long finger of Cap Corse and the compact mountain block of Castagniccia, together occupying the northeastern corner of the island, and which stretch in a narrowing band as far south as Solenzara. The GR20, though in close proximity east of Monte Incudine, does not seriously impinge on this area, but follows in stylish fashion the true watershed ridge of the Island - so well expressed by the French version: 'la Gande Ligne de Partage des Eaux'. The other routes described in this volume, notably Walks 1 and 2, do cross a narrow band of folded schists.

## Flora

Anyone unfamiliar with the nature of Corsica, more attuned to the open aspect of the UK, and other parts of highland Europe, may wonder why these paths require such a specific degree of physical development particularly as there used to be a complex interlacing of mule tracks and shepherds' paths of transhumance throughout the island. The difficulty is caused by the all-pervading maquis, the unique scrub vegetation that grows in varying density and height in any and every open space, but with greatest exuberance below 600 metres. Maquis can also be found at its impenetrable worst under the thick cover of old chestnut trees, and less densely in forest clearings and on plateaux at heights of 1,500 metres. The principal shrubs are arbutus lentisk, myrtle, cistus, and numerous forms of broom, erica and gorse, interlaced with other

Col de Bavella

spiny forms. At higher altitudes there is considerable ground cover of scrub alder, dwarf juniper and assorted aromatics like rosemary, lavender, and thyme. The semi-wild pigs and boars can tunnel their way through it, but for walkers it is mostly impenetrable, and at its highest and densest is to be avoided at all costs.

The maquis is a partially degraded form of vegetation that has spread over previously cultivated areas at low level and invaded higher slopes where fire has destroyed great forest areas. It gives off a strange, haunting, bitter-sweet perfume that Napoleon wrote about nostalgically during his exile, and in early spring is ablaze with wild flowers. It is also the reason why so much effort was required by the Parc Naturel, clearing and marking old paths and mule tracks fallen into disuse, to create new coast-to-coast and other long-distance walks.

One will not find in Corsica vast acres of flower-filled meadows, as in the Pyrénées, nor the massed crocus and gentians that grow on the limestone mountains of northern Greece. Wild flowers are plentiful enough in the spring, but there is no hint of lushness in the mountain pastures (see also page 113).

## Food

The local food of Corsica is not, to my knowledge, specially rated for either variety or quality. The coastal resorts, of course, provide the usual Mediterranean fare at the usual inflated prices for tourists. The GR20, however, provides little opportunity, outside Calenzana and Vizzavona, to sample the local fare which is mainly celebrated for its charcuterie - a large assortment of products from the very same pigs encountered everywhere, and which prevent re-generation of the ageing beech and chestnut forests. Sheep and goats most commonly provide cheese - cheese-making is still the main summer occupation of the shepherds.

The local village inns at least maintain the splendid French tradition of very good home-made soup in generous quantities, and the dishes of wild rabbit and locally caught trout are invariably excellent. The local wine, said to be improving in quality, can be first rate but is variable. I personally have to admit to a weakness for the Hotel Moderne in Vizzavona, which used to cater for British ex-patriates in the late 19th and early 20th century with ballroom, log fires, and a forest skating rink. Unaltered, perhaps verging on the romantically seedy, it offers the best indigenous menu at the most reasonable cost that I have encountered in the island, and keeps a superbly stocked grocery at a critical point on the GR20 (see also page 68).

### British Mountaineers in Corsica

When planning a route it may be of interest that, besides British political links with Corsica in the 18th century some of the earliest mountaineering records concerning Corsica are also in English. The second recorded ascent of Monte Cinto, the highest peak, was by the English Alpinist Tuckett, accompanied by the mountaineer-painter Compton, and a French guide, F. Devouassoud, in May 1883. In the same period Tuckett and the more famous alpinist and Himalayan pioneer Douglas Freshfield, were also exploring the regions of Bavella and Incudine (Alpine Journal, Vol. X). As Michel Fabriquant, the ultimate authority on Corsican mountains, stated in his definitive `Guide des Montagnes Corses' (Didier & Richard 1982) that not until 1927 was the Bavella region again visited by mountaineers.

Fabriquant also records that George Finch, his brother Maxwell, and the Norwegian Bryn made the first true alpine ascent of Paglia Orba, by the east face on the 15 April 1909 in almost winter conditions. It is still considered to be one of the great exploits of Corsican mountaineering. It must have been a remarkable spring since in the same month this party also climbed the Capu a u Dente above the Col de Tartagine, and made the first complete traverse of the Cinque Frati, that remarkable toothed ridge to the east of the Grotte des Anges. These small items of British pioneering might add a little zest, even a little piquancy perhaps, as you stand, exhausted in mind and body, on the Bocca Minuta astride the Grande Barriere, with the Col de la Solitude either behind you - or yet to be crossed!

What, if anything, makes walking in Corsica such a special experience? Previous writers have used well-known phrases to describe the island like `the scented isle' and `Ile de beaute'. The ancient Greeks called it `Kalliste' - the most beautiful. To see its towered and spired granite peaks rising clear of the gigantic laricio pine forest, snow still white on their highest crags and their steep red cliffs falling to a turquoise sea, is to know that Corsica is quite unlike any other Mediterranean island.

For myself I often think of a remote bergerie of the Niolo, not far from the Lac de Nino, where once I passed a moonlit night. The Rotondo massif lay spread across the southern horizon, bathed in phosphorescent light, ice bound and shimmering like some distant Antarctic coastline. I recognised the place at once from Dorothy Carrington's description of it: `I lay awake as long as I could for the deep satisfaction of seeing fire flicker against the rough surfaced granite, the huge deformed shadows of the men when they rose to feed it, the white ghost shapes of the rocks through the open door, under a moon, and a sheet of snow on the opposite mountainside .... I had an almost physical sensation of being drawn down and back to the roots of humanity, to my lost origins, in a dream more comforting than any I have ever known in sleep' (from Granite Island, Penguin). Such experiences are rarely to be found within the peopled confines of a refuge. They are indigenous to the bivvy in bergerie, cave, or under fallen trees. They are the very essence of Corsica and the reason for going back.

# WALK 1

### Calenzana
🏠 ⌂ ⅄ ✕ ⅄ 🚊 🚌 🅿

*275m*

*(Map ref A)*

*Situated 12 kilometres southeast of Calvi, the principal small town of the Balagne, precisely below Monte Grosso; a place of substance with several squares and winding narrow streets climbing steeply to the south; the most important, and most westerly of the villages along the corniche high above the once richly farmed lands of the Balagne; said to have been the home base of many of the Corsican expatriate mobsters of Marseilles.*

1:00

### Carrefour de Sentiers
*550m*

*The GR20 divides into the Low Level route to the southwest and the Alternative High Level route to the south.*

The signposted route of the GR20 follows the main road past the Monte Grosso Hotel, branching to the right at the main Church Square, and climbs directly uphill to the upper part of the village. A sharp turn right along a level narrow street, past a small bar on the left, leads to a small courtyard, Place St. Antoine, that at first appears to be a cul de sac, in the southwest corner of the village. Faded red and white waymark flashes and a timber sign of Le Parc Naturel Règional de la Corse (PNRC) indicate the start of the GR and of Walk 2 along a narrow old lane overhung by domestic gardens. To the right, and at a slightly lower level as you leave the courtyard, there is an old covered public wash place, with good water. The GR follows an old mulepath winding up around the side of a subsidiary hill and turning more directly southwest. A steady ascent through scattered pine trees, above lower beech groves and abandoned terraces, leads up past the Fontaine d'Ortivinti to the Carrefour de Sentiers, identified by a standard Park sign.

From the junction there are 2 alternative routes to the Refuge de Carozzu, close to Spasimata:

1. The low level route to the southwest which, as far as Bocca Reza also forms the first stage of Walk 2, `Strada tra mare e monti'. Spasimata is reached beyond Bonifatu by taking the old GR20 from Roncu, the junction of the Melaghia and Ficarella Streams. This path is now marked with orange flashes throughout, although faded red and white GR20 marks are still occasionally visible above Roncu. It presents little difficulty and is practicable in all seasons.

2. The other alternative swings left, to the south, to form a newly established GR20 High Level route following the ridge of Capu Ghiovu, 1637 metres. This route follows steep ground with several rock passages, slightly exposed, but assisted by fixed cables. It is a very demanding route in hot weather, with no obvious water

after starting the climb.

**Warning** It is a route to be avoided in conditions of snow, or threatening electric storms.

**Junction**
**Carrefour de Sentiers**

**Low Level Alternative GR20:** Carrefour de Sentiers to the Refuge de Carozzu by the Auberge de Bonifatu. From the junction follow the track waymarked orange to the west as far as the Bocca a Corsu at 581 metres. There is a magnificent view back to Calenzana and the other elevated villages of the Balagne. The GR turns south following the ancient `Postman's path', descends towards the ruined Bergerie de Sambucca, crosses a stream with a small open pool and winds its way through chest-high maquis to a stone-white forestry road. Continue downhill on the forestry road, passing a fresh water spring on the left, through an area denuded by fire and submerged in dense maquis to a substantial concrete bridge over the Ficarella at 360 metres. Cross the bridge to the true left bank and continue more or less alongside the river, occasionally impeded by maquis and partially burnt fallen trees. Turning sharply uphill to the right, in a series of short hairpin bends the path joins the D251 Calvi to Bonifatu road at Bocca Reza.

3:00

**Bocca Reza**
*513m*
*Walk 2, `Strada tra mare e monti' crosses the D251 and climbs in a westerly direction towards the Bocca di Bonassa to Galeria.*

0:30

The Low Level GR20 continues along the D251, passing the maison forestière, to the Auberge de Bonifatu.

**AUBERGE DE BONIFATU**
*540m*
⌂ ⌂ Å ✕ ♨

0:20

From the auberge car park take the GR along the forestry road to Roncu.

**Roncu**
*620m*
*Beautiful place, where Melaghia and Lamitu streams join to form Ficarella river; situated in magnificent forest and much visited by tourists.*

**Detour,**
**REFUGE L'ORTU DI U**
**PIOBBU**
*1,570m*

**2:15**

**Detour** see left. Take the forestry road on the left that runs north and then northeast directly up the Melaghia valley for approximately 3.5 kilometres. From the nearby stream-crossing an ancient mule path climbs in long sweeping hairpins through a pine forest to a sloping open plateau due west of the Bocca di Tartagine. On reaching more open country, at approximately 1,200 metres, the track, marked by small cairns, turns sharply in a southwesterly direction and ascends to the hut, where walkers can join the High Level Alternative GR20 from Piobbu to Carozzu.

From Roncu follow the path, an old, well-used mule track, which continues, steeply at first, through forest keeping to the true left bank of the Lamitu stream. Approximately 2.5 kilometres above Roncu, at 910 metres, cross to the right bank by boulder hopping - accomplished fairly easily in average conditions. It is important after the crossing to turn to the right, parallel to the stream, and follow the orange marked track towards Carozzu.

**Warning** A small cairned path ascends away from the stream to provide a steep climber's access to the crags above. Should you find yourself on steepening slabs where a rope might be thought appropriate, you are definitely on the wrong path.

The fairly steep track through trees opens out after approximately 1 kilometre providing splendid views of the Spasimata ravine. An old stone hut marks the site of Spasimata.

**Spasimata**
*1,190m*

**0:15**

A short climb up to the left in steep hairpin bends leads to the Refuge de Carozzu.

**REFUGE DE CAROZZU**
🏠 ⛺
*1,260m*
*The Low Level GR20 joins*
*the High Level Alternative*
*route from Calenzana.*

**Junction
Carrefour de Sentiers**

**2:30**

**Boccu u Saltu**
*1,250m*
*Dramatic view down into the
great western cirque and
the protected forest of
Monte Grosso.*

*As late as July small trickles
of water provide sustenance
for a profusion of wild
flowers among the rocks on*
**2:50**
*the barren scree slopes that
drop dramatically into the
forest far below.*

**High Level Alternative GR20:** Carrefour de Sentiers to the Refuge de Carozzu by the Refuge l'Orto di u Piobbu. From the junction the route swings left around the base of a rock pinnacle and takes a contouring but generally rising line towards the southeast, well above the re-planted terraces. The path crosses several small springs until the larger Arghioa stream is reached. Note that this water source, normally available until August, is the last supply en route to the Refuge d'Orto di u Piobbu. Ignore the faint red and white waymarks of the old GR20 route still visible on the same approximate line towards the Santucce. The new ridge route turns sharply left, to the east, on a steep line to follow a shallow gully towards the skyline ridge. This path, badly graded and consequently much eroded, through scattered pines and rocks, is a hard climb of 500 metres to the open broad col of Boccu u Saltu.

The path, crossing the col, drops down into the upper reaches of the Monte Grosso Cirque taking first a descending and ultimately a rising line across the northeast face of Capu Ghiovu. Starting as an easy forest track the route eventually takes a fairly complex line high across the rock gullies and buttresses of the main summit. Fixed cables are in position at various exposed situations, but some may consider a plastic-coated wire cable more of a hindrance than a help when grasped by a sweaty palm.

**Warning** This passage on rock is of a serious scrambling nature and occasionally the route is not obvious so that you must look for the waymarks ahead. Walkers, inexperienced in route finding across complex rock formations, must ensure that they stay on route. An unfamiliar load encourages imbalance on awkward passages and any kind of fall in this situation is likely to be serious. These remarks apply equally to later sections of the route.

From a subsidiary col south of Capu Ghiovu an easier line is followed to the south, rising to cross the head of the southwesterly ridge above the Bergerie de Santucci, from where, at about 1,500 metres, the path contours in a great arc around the head of the Melaghia Valley. A slight descent into a small ravine, among alder scrub and birch trees, leads to a junction, the old track rising left to the Boca di Tartagine, but the GR turns right along the steep gully side and rises on a left hand curve on to the plateau and the Refuge l'Orto di u Piobbu.

## REFUGE L'ORTO DI U PIOBBU
⌂

*1,570m*

The ancient mule track that crosses the Bocca di Tartagine can be joined where it descends the sloping plateau below the refuge, and from where the Auberge de Bonifatu and the Low Level Alternative GR20 can be reached in 2 hrs 30 mins. The track is marked by small cairns until it enters the lower forest area, where it becomes obvious.

**3:00**

*There is an additional water source at Piobbu, a few yards down the GR20 to Carozzu situated among birch trees.*

The GR20 heads southwest, climbing steadily through birch forest before it swings back to the southeast after crossing a ridge at 1,627 metres. It descends towards the ruined Bergerie of Mandriaccia, and crosses the Mandriaccia stream at 1,469 metres. The path continues up the long couloir to the south, climbing to a col at approximately 2,000 metres, east of Punta Pisciaghia, and crosses onto the south face of Capu Ladruncellu. A climbing traverse among rocks, in describing an arc from east to south, leads to the Col d'Avartoli.

## Col d'Avartoli
*1,898m*
*The rock scenery here is some of the finest in Corsica and looking ahead to try and identify ridges and cols still to be crossed can be confusing since frequently the scale and precipitous nature of the surrounding landscape defies belief that there is a relatively safe way ahead. The red and white flashes are reassuring.*

**1:30**

Following the ridge line south from d'Avartoli you encounter several delicate rock scrambling passages before the route leaves the ridge line and turns southwest to the right to reach yet another col almost due west of Punta Ghialla. This, the Col de l'Inominata, 1,912 metres, is a brèche on the massive western spur of Ghialla which separates the Ravines of Ladruncellu and Carozzu. A very steep and rocky descent of the southern couloir leads to the stream supplying the old Carozzu Bergerie. Follow the stream through occasional hairpins to the refuge, close by the old Bergerie.

## REFUGE DE CAROZZU
⌂Å

*1,260m*

From the refuge the GR20 descends to the southwest and crosses the Spasimata torrent by a suspended footbridge to the true left bank.

*(Map ref B)*
*The High Level Alternative*
*GR20 joins the Low Level*
*Alternative route from*
*Bonifatu.*

**3:00**

Proceeding upstream the walker soon encounters the notorious inclined slabs which are traversed by way of horizontal, and sometimes sloping, grooves and delicate ledges.

**Warning** There is need of balance and good friction for the feet so that the slabs should not be attempted in wet weather. There is some cable assistance across the most exposed sections. Certainly this passage, which is continuous for some distance, should be treated with great caution.

Beyond the slabs, at a confluence of streams, at 1,464 metres, the track, veering to the left in a southeasterly direction, starts the real climb out of the Spasimata Ravine. The ascent of this glacial cwm steepens as you clamber up rocky ribs and intervening gullies which in places are heavily infested by the all pervasive scrub alder. The steeper sections are assisted by fixed cables. The track then reaches a high glaciated hollow that contains the Lac de la Muvrella.

**Lac de la Muvrella**
*1,860m*
*Litter problem in this vicinity*
*with plans to clear the lake*
*of rubbish; at present water*
*is considerably polluted*
*and undrinkable.*
**Detour,**
*Summit of the Muvrella*

**Detour** see left. The summit of the Muvrella can be reached from this point by following a path marked by double yellow flashes. The line of the GR20 is rejoined by descending the south ridge from the summit.

The GR20 climbs to the south from the lake by way of a broad couloir. The thickets of dwarf alder give way to bouldery scree; the path reaches the ridge above by a little brèche, 2,000 metres high, between rocky pinnacles and crosses the brèche, situated on a subsidiary ridge west of Muvrella, on to the southwest face.

**1:30**

*The highly dramatic view*
*extends down into the great*

The main watershed ridge, south of Muvrella, is gained by a contouring path which bends

*ravine of Maghine and even further to the distant Fango valley.*

to the south until Punta Stranciacone and Missoghiu are directly ahead. The path follows the ridge at an average altitude of 2,000 metres passing the Bocca Culaghia, 1,957 metres, with a rise over the punta Culaghia.

**Punta Culaghia**
*2,034m*

From the summit the ridge path, diverging slightly to the southwest, descends for a distance of approximately 300 metres to a little col at 1,980 metres. The path leaves the ridge and making a sharp left turn, to the east, descends very steeply to the ski station/hotel at Haut Asco.

1:30

**Bocca Culaghia**

**Alternative route** from the Bocca Culaghia to the Old Refuge d'Altore. The present marked route of the GR down to Haut Asco is a variation from the original and has been established since the burning down of the refuge d'Altore in 1985. There was always a yellow marked old path, from north of the Bocca Culaghia, down to Haut Asco, but the line of the GR proper originally continued south beyond the Col at 1,980 metres and contoured below and to the west of the Punta Stranciacone. From a deep col between Stranciacone and Missoghiu a steep descent to the southeast led directly to a track contouring the head of the Asco Valley at 1,880 metres. For anyone not wishing to sacrifice the height loss down to Haut Asco, and prepared to bivouac in the region of the old d'Altore refuge, the original route directly to the head of the valley is still the most economical alternative.

**HAUT ASCO**
**(Refuge de Stagnu)**
Ⓗ ⌂ ✕ ⚓
*1,422m*

From the ski station at Haut Asco the GR ascends the valley, following an old moraine, to an intermediate plateau. The route is well above the true left bank of the main valley stream, but also keeps the winter ski run well to the right in order to avoid an arduous ascent on scree slopes. Passing below the eastern slopes of Punta Missoghiu the present GR rejoins the older contouring track, among alder brush, around the head of the main valley. After passing the foot of the Bocca Stranciacone a basin, much glaciated and surrounded by slopes covered in reddish scree, is reached at 1,930 metres. A short climb leads up a stony ridge, a northern spur of Pic von Cube, to the

2:00

### Old Refuge d'Altore

*2,000m*
*Reasonable bivouac places in the vicinity of the old refuge in the shelter of its walls although an exposed place in bad weather; no shortage of water. A likely area on the GR route where mouflon can be sighted - always in the early morning.*

**0:35**

### Col Perdu

*2,183m*
*The Cirque de la Solitude is a classical hanging valley, high upon the western face of the main watershed ridge and the route across it is properly considered to be the crux of the northern section of the GR20. It has a reputation for being the most technically difficult passage of the entire route.*

*This is a magnificent and awesome place but in high season is likely to be very popular.*

**1:45**

### Bocca Minuta

*2,218m*
*Second highest col on the*

site of the old Refuge d'Altore.

From the site of the old refuge a steady ascent to the southeast, on the line of two small lakes brings you to the threshold of the Cirque de la Solitude at the Col Perdu.

The crossing of the cirque, which provides a 205 metres descent and a 240 metre re-ascent, involves a high degree of exposure upon steep rocks. But in following the marked route carefully, and taking full advantage of the fixed cables, little actual technical difficulty is encountered.

**Warning** Due to the likely proximity of other persons try never to dislodge loose rock or even small stones which can be equally lethal after a 200 metre free fall. The cirque is of course a place to avoid completely in very bad weather, particularly when electric storms are a possibility.

The descent from the Col Perdu is steep but well supplied with fixed assistance. The path leads down by a scree filled gully to the lowest part from where a steeply rising traverse across slabs, frequently running with water but again protected by handrail cables, gives access to an even steeper recessed couloir which eventually, lessening in gradient, brings one to the Bocca Minuta.

The descent to the south from Bocca Minuta is rough, fairly steep and much encumbered by awkward rocks and slabs. Descending

*GR20. On the Bocca Minuta you stand, however, briefly, upon that part of the main watershed ridge known as the Grande Barrière, that runs from Punta Minuta in the north to Paglia Orba in the south. The traverse of this compact ridge of many summits is one of the great climbing classics in Corsica.*

1:30

## REFUGE TIGHJETTU
⌂
*1,640m*

0:30

## BERGERIES DE BALLONE
🔺 ⍾
*1,440m*
*(Map ref C)*
*A good water supply.*

1:30

## CALASIMA
✕ ⛲
*1,095m*
**Detour,**
## ALBERTACCE
⌂
*and*
## CALACUCCIA
🏠 ⌂ ✕ ⍾ ⛲

3:00

down the true left bank of the ravin du Stranciacone, and a little above its confluence with the ravin de Valle di Stagni, you arrive at the Refuge Tighjettu.

A further descent from the refuge, continuing downstream brings you to the Bergeries de Ballone.

**Alternative route** from the Bergeries de Ballone to Calasima avoiding the ascent to the Col de Foggiale and the Refuge Ciottulu di i Mori at 2,000 metres. From the bergeries take the path to the southeast, on the left bank of the river Viro (or Viru) signposted to La Grotte des Anges and from there a forestry road to Calasima, a total distance of approximately 5.5 kilometres.

**Detour** see left. Follow the D318 road - either on foot or by taxi - to Albertacce and from there to Calacuccia.

To rejoin the GR20 take the path, marked with orange flashes, from the D318 road to the south of the village descending to the southwest among chestnut trees. It crosses the Viro by a metal bridge and re-ascends among trees to a little col at 1,115 metres, where there is a junction. Take the left branch, to the south, and after a slight descent the path bends in a southwesterly direction to follow the contour at approximately 1,100 metres, for 2 kilometres. It crosses the Castellu stream at the point marked 1,149 metres and ascends to

approximately 1,200 metres continuing on this contour to re-enter the forest. About 2 kilometres after crossing the Castellu the route follows a forestry road which ultimately descends south to the Golo Valley. The forestry road is followed for a short distance, about 300 metres, before regaining, to the right, the original path which again contours before rising progressively to traverse an open area at 1,250 metres, passing the di e Noci Spring before rejoining the main GR20 on the left bank of the Golo river at the Cascade de Radule.

### BERGERIES DE BALLONE
Å Ψ
*1,440m*
*(Map ref C)*
*A good water supply.*

**2:45**

From the Bergeries de Ballone the GR20 follows the true right bank of the Viro and contours at approximately 1,400 metres around the base of the east face of Paglia Orba, through a forest, partially destroyed by fire, of Laricco pines some 350-400 years old. Crossing the bottom of a forested ridge, southeast of Paglia Orba, the GR joins an old path, from the Bergerie de Prugnoli, that climbs westward out of the Foce Ghiallu Valley. A steep ascent of 560 metres on rocky terrain leads up to the Col de Fogghiale.

### Col de Fogghiale
*1,962m*
*Referred to as Bocca di Foghieghiallu on the IGN map.*

**0:20**

The route crosses the col and bearing northwest, climbs across a sloping plateau covered in maquis. At the base of the west face of Capu Tafonatu, close to the Golo spring, the path reaches the Refuge Ciottulu di i Mori.

**Alternative route.** If there is no intention of stopping at the Refuge take a route southwest across the lower part of the plateau, direct from the Col de Fogghiale to the Bergeries de Tula, 1,700 metres where there should always be water.

### Refuge Ciottulu di i Mori
*2,000m*
*This Refuge is very often occupied by climbers.*

From the Refuge the GR, in describing an arc to the west, follows for approximately 600 metres the line of the ridge forming the western side of the upper Golo Valley, sometimes referred to as the `Vallon de Tula'. At 1,907 metres the path turns left to descend over rocky ground and poor pasture to the old shepherd's path on the right bank of the Golo stream, a little below the Bergerie de Tula at 1,700 metres.

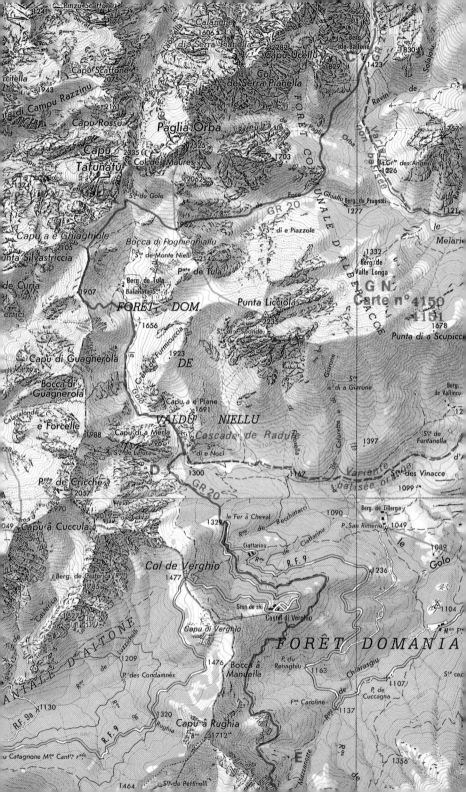

**1:20**

*It is much easier, and shorter, to descend directly down the valley to this point from the Refuge, but the ridge route provides unique views to the west and is highly recommended.*

Continuing down the right bank the GR20 is shortly joined from the right by the ancient path of 'transhumance' Filosorma - Niolo, along which seasonal migration of men, horses, sheep and goats was made from the low level western valleys over the Bocca di Guagnerola to the mountain pastures of the Niolo region. Below this junction the path crosses to the true left bank of the steam at 1,544 metres, a place where there are good pools for bathing. Below this point, by way of a very rough and stony ravine the GR reaches the Cascade de Radule.

**Detour,** *45 mins.*
**CASTEL DI VERGHIO**
🏠 🍴 ⛲
*1,404m*

**Detour** see left. From the Bergeries de Radule a faint track waymarked yellow goes uphill to the Col de Verghio. Turn left at the RF9 road and walk down the road to Castel di Verghio.

**Cascade de Radule**
*1,370m*
*(Map ref D)*
*The orange waymarked alternative track from Calasima, joins the GR20 on the left.*

**0:30**

Upstream from the Cascade de Radule the GR20 turns right, crossing the stream, to pass through the rather unusual Bergeries de Radule - Gratule on the IGN maps, from where a fairly horizontal track passes into the forest of Valdu Niellu to reach the RF9 road at a large 'horse-shoe' bend, known as the 'Fer-à-Cheval'.

**Fer-à-Cheval**
*1,329m*
*Walk 2 'Sermano-Corte-Cargese' intersects the GR20 near the Ciatterina barracks approximately 1 kilometre from Fer-à-Cheval.*
**Detour,** *30 mins.*
**CASTEL DI VERGHIO**
🏠 🍴 ⛲
*1,404m*

**Detour** see left. Walk up the RF9 road on the right from the Fer-à-Cheval for approximately 2 kilometres to Castel di Verghio.

*Between Verghio and Vizzavona there is no practical possibility of replenishing food supplies other than by making long diversions to Orto or to Canaglia or by making use of the hotel facilities at Castel di Verghio.*

**2:25**

From the Fer-à-Cheval, walk along the RF9 for a short distance to a good path through the forest of Valdu Niellu that follows the contour, first to the east and then by a large bend, to the southwest. The GR crosses several small streams until, close to a spring, it encounters the 'link path' climbing back up to Castel di Verghio.

**Detour,** *30 mins.*
**CASTEL DI VERGHIO**

The old mule track continues at precisely the same altitude through the forest, contouring

◻ ✕ 🪑
*1,404m*
*A yellow marked `link path'
climbs up directly through
the forest from the 1,332
metre point to Castel di
Verghio.*

### Col de Saint-Pierre
*1,452m*
*(Map ref E)*

2:00

### Lac de Nino
*1,743m*
*Around the lake open grass
pastures slope gently down
to the shores with areas of
peaty turf, known locally as
`pozzines' or `tourbières'.
Cattle and horses grazing
create a peaceful
atmosphere, with a distant
view down the upper
Tavignano valley to the
great Monte Rotondo
massif. Camping is totally
forbidden in this area.*

2:00

### Bocca d'Acqua Ciarnente
*1,568m*
*(Map ref F)*

around every obstruction for a total distance of approximately 7 kilometres. At a crossing of paths the GR20 turns right and climbs to the upper limits of a beech wood onto the Col de Saint-Pierre.

At the col the GR joins an ancient mule track, coming from the west which climbs in well graded hairpin bends on to the crest of San Tomaghiu, diverges to the left off the ridge across the head of a couloir, and rises once more in hairpins back to the ridge proper at the 1,816 metre point. From this ridge there is a fine view to the north of the Cinto, Tafunatu and Paglia Orba ranges beyond the foreground forest of the Valdu Niellu. The path cuts across the southern slopes of Capu a u Lozzu to the Bocca Redda (Bocca a Reta on the IGN map) at 1,883 metres, and from there descends steadily down to the northwest corner of the Lac de Nino.

The GR20 follows the general direction of the Tavignano stream which has its source in the lake. At a sharp bend in the stream where it flows round a rocky barrier, below the Bergerie d'Insecche, the GR route turns right in a southeasterly direction deviating from the old mule path, marked yellow, which continues in the direction of Corte. The GR takes a line progressively more distant from the Tavignano, and crosses a secondary stream, to pass through a large flat area on the edge of what remains of the beech forest of Campotile at 1,597 metres. From the site of the old Refuge de Campiglioni, and after passing through the remains of the beech forest, the track still heading slightly east of south over easy ground reaches the Bergerie of Vaccaghia at 1,621 metres and where in season cheese is generally for sale. The GR makes a gentle descent across open prairie on to the line of the main watershed at the Bocca d'Acqua Ciarnente.

**Detour,** *2 hrs*
**ORTO**
⚒

0:15    *700m 3 hrs return and*
**SOCCIA**
⚒
*729m*

**Detour** see left. From the Bocca d'Acqua Ciarnente a path, yellow waymarked, goes west down to Lac de Creno. After about 30 minutes walking from the lake, for Orto, take the left fork at the junction, or the right fork for Soccia.

Maintaining a southerly direction from the col the GR makes a short climb up to the Manganu stream and the nearby Refuge de Manganu.

**REFUGE DE MANGANU**
⌂ �

*1,601m*
*The refuge is on the opposite bank of the stream and is approached over a bridge.*

2:45

The next passage across the Rotondo massif to Pietra Piana and beyond, as far as Vizzavona, is of an arduous nature and, in places, almost as spectacular as the Cirque de la Solitude. On the same bearing, slightly east of south, the GR ascends the true right bank of the Manganu stream through alternate areas of exposed rock ribs and vegetation until, crossing the lower threshold of a large cirque, a small lake is encountered at 1,969 metres. The path turns east, and makes a long and rough climb up the back of the facing couloir. It steepens towards the top and reaches the main watershed of the island at the Brèche de Capitello, one of the many brèches that punctuate the line of Aiguilles running like a series of blunt needles along the ridge.

**Warning** Even in high summer, snow is likely to remain on the slopes immediately east of the Brèche de Capitello. It is likely to be granular spring snow and dangerous to the unwary, and particularly to those inexperienced in snow conditions. This very exposed section of the route therefore necessitates the greatest care.

**Brèche de Capitello**
*2,225m*
*Highest point on the GR20.*
*From the Brèche de Capitello the surrounding peaks of the Punta alle Porte, immediately to the*
1:15    *right on crossing the Brèche, Punta Capitello, and Lombarduccio dominate a great hollow to the west, containing at*

On leaving the Brèche the route descends across a slope above Lac Capitello, to the southeast until, south of the lake and due east of Punta alle Porte you rejoin the main ridge at a small gap. It is possible to descend the gully below this gap to the lake, on a route waymarked yellow. A pinnacle marks the point where the GR20 threads its way along the south side of the ridge as it descends to reach the Bocca Soglia.

*different levels Lac Capitello and Lac de Melo.*

### Bocca Soglia
*2,052m*

1:10

From this broad col, due south of Lac de Melo, the route turns in an arc to the left, running northeast more or less horizontally across the northwest face of the main watershed peak of Mozzello until it ends at the foot of a steep slope covered in alder scrub. Turning right, to the east, you climb among rocks and alder to a shallow nick, on a northern spur of the Mozzello, the Col de Rinoso.

### Col de Rinoso
*2,150m*

0:20

On the other side of the col the GR passes above and to the right of the little Lac de Rinoso, to follow a line south of east among bouldery slabs, heavy infestations of alder and juniper until, rising steadily across the northeast slopes of Mozzello, it reaches the Col de la Haute Route.

### Col de la Haute Route
*2,206m*
*Situated on the island's main watershed and the third highest point crossed in the course of the GR.*

1:00

On the southern side of the col the GR20 continues in a southeast direction, semi contouring across slopes southwest of the minor summit of Maniccia in order to cross the ridge that runs due south from the same summit. The point of crossing at approximately 2,050 metres is some distance to the north of the Col de Manganello, 1,800 metres, which, in clear weather, is visible from above. A descent to the east brings you to a small ledge or plateau and, situated among alder scrub, the Refuge de Pietra Piana.

### REFUGE DE PIETRA PIANA
⌂ ⚑
*1,842m*
**Detour,** *5 hrs*
**Monte Rotondo**
*2,622m*

**Detour** see left. From the refuge ascend, slightly east of north, cross an ancient lake bed at 1,960 metres and continue northeast. Climb steep couloir leading to a brèche above, and beyond, to a great hollow which contains the Lac de Monte Rotondo. From the lake, in an east-northeast direction, a steep climb up scree leads to a deep col distinguished by an isolated pinnacle - the Col du Fer de Lance. Turning left at the col an easy scramble up the ridge leads to the summit, where there is a small shelter.

*(Map ref G)*

South of the Refuge de Pietra Piana there are two alternative routes to the Refuge de l'Onda, close to the col d'Oreccia: the `high level' route and the `valley' route.

1. The high level route is shorter in distance than the valley route with a gain in time of 45 minutes going from north to south, and 30 minutes in the reverse direction. It also provides a minimum gain or loss in height.

**Warning** In threatening weather and particularly when visibility is bad, the high level route should be avoided.

2. The valley route, although longer, takes one through superb forest and by some of the finest stretches of torrent in Corsica. It is a route of great variety as it descends over open rocky terrain and small waterfalls to the depth of the forest and the grandeur of the Manganello cascades. Moreover it offers the possibility of leaving the GR, a little below the bergeries de Tolla, where a minor road leads to the village of Canaglia and thence to the N193 and railway station at Tattone.

**REFUGE DE PIETRA PIANA**
△ Ⴔ
*1,842m*

0:30

**High Level Alternative Route** to the Refuge de l'Onda. From the Refuge de Pietra Piana the marked track to the southwest descends to 1,750 metres and, continuing in the same direction, re-ascends to a break in the ridge, slightly north of the Bocca Manganello, from where it follows, in the grand manner, the ridge to the south to the Bocca Manganello.

**Bocca Manganello**
*1,800m*
**Detour,** *3 hrs*
**GUAGNO**
ⓗ ⚒
*750m*
*4 hrs 30 mins return*

1:30

**Detour** see left. From the Bocca Manganello descend to the southwest by a path on the true left bank of the Flume Grosso Stream.

From the Bocca Manganello continue south along the ridge to the Pointe de Pinzi Corbini.

**Pointe de Pinzi Corbini**
*2,021m*

The path, descending again, crosses the Bocca alla Meta at 1,890 metres and, on leaving the col, moves off the ridge on to the northeast slope which is traversed towards a brèche marked by two trees. The brèche is reached

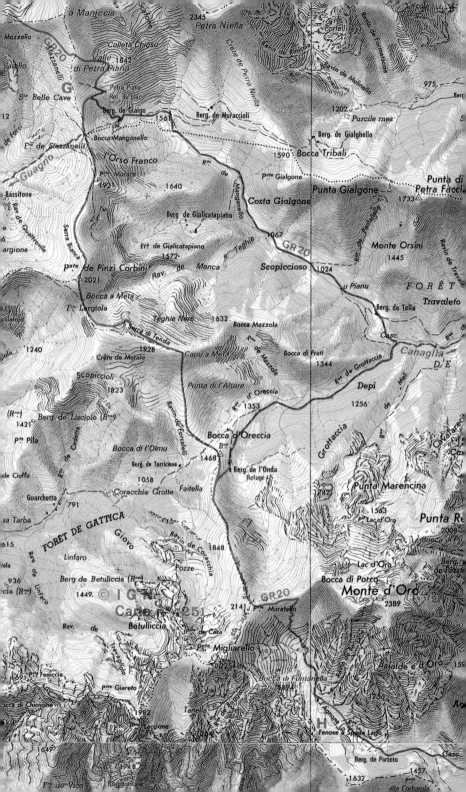

by a steep little climb. From the brèche the track, now heading in a southeasterly direction, moves across to the southern side of the ridge proper, and descends gradually towards the Bocca d'Oreccia.

## Bocca d'Oreccia

*1,427m*
*The alternative valley route joins the High Level Route.*
**Detour,** *5 hrs*

## Chiusa

*700m*
*From the col a track leaves the GR on the right to Chiusa.*

From the Col d'Oreccia, after a short climb by way of a grassy ridge at 1,468 metres, the alternative valley route from Tolla is joined and a brief descent to the left leads to the Refuge de l'Onda.

## REFUGE DE PIETRA PIANA

⌂ ⚠
*1,842m*

**Valley Alternative Route** to the Refuge de l'Onda. From the Refuge the path is common to both alternatives, but the valley route deviates to the southeast to the bergeries de Gialgo at 1,609 metres from where, going more directly east, it joins the old access track to the bergeries. The GR leaves this old track, with traces of formerly well maintained steps, at the junction by the Manganello stream at 1,440 metres.

While the old shepherd's track carries on to the east, the GR20 goes right, descending towards the southeast and staying on the true left bank of the Manganello. The path varies in width before it enters the forest where eventually it becomes a rough forest access road. The deep pools and the water slides of the Manganello remain on the right. The old road reverts to a footpath before reaching the Bergerie de Tolla at 1,011 metres where cheese is often available. From the bergerie a bridge crosses to the right bank of the Manganello.

## The Manganello Bridge

*930m*
*The bridge is slightly downstream of the junction of the Manganello and the Grottacia streams.*
**Detour,** *1 hr*

## CANAGLIA

✕ 🍷

**Detour**. From the bridge take the good works road to the left which follows the general direction of the Manganello for 4 kilometres to

2:00

3:00

1:40

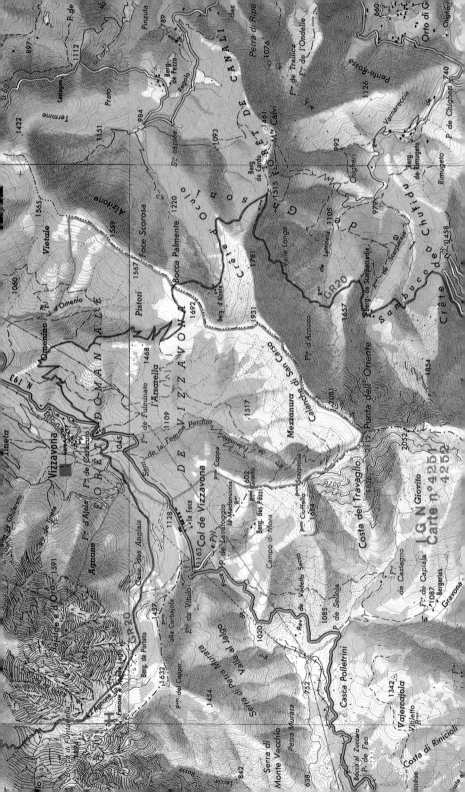

720m
**TATTONE**
✕ ⚒ ▄▄
*further 1 hr 15 mins*

**REFUGE DE L'ONDA**
◯ ⋀
*1,430m*
*The Bergerie nearby sells*
*cheese in season. The*
*Alternative High Level Route*
*joins the Alternative Valley*
*Route.*

2:20

**The Muratello Ridge**
*2,020m*

0:20

**Junction, Monte d'Oro**
**west**
*2,000m*
*From this junction it is*
*possible to take in the*
*summit of Monte d'Oro en*
*route to Vizzavona.*
**Warning** *Not advisable in*
*threatening weather*
*conditions.*

5:00

**Junction, Monte d'Oro**
**west**

Canaglia. Tattone is a further 3 kilometres by the D23 road from Canaglia.
The GR20 re-ascends to the southwest up the right hand bank of the Grottacia, crosses the stream and after passing below a beech wood reaches the Bergeries de l'Onda and the nearby Refuge del'Onda.

From the refuge the GR20 follows the long ridge south to the Punta Muratello. It is a continuous climb, without respite, until the path reaches the east-west ridge that joins the Punta Muratello, at 2,141 metres, to Monte d'Oro, 2,389 metres.

The path follows the ridge which now turns east, towards the summit of Monte d'Oro. It continues, generally on the south side, bypassing any difficulties, for about 500 metres to a junction. At the junction the GR makes a sharp turn to the right to start the rough descent into the upper basin of the Agnone, and is joined on the left by a path from the ridge to the east.

**Alternative route.** Take the path which continues to the east along the ridge soon rising in a northeasterly direction as far as the Bocca di Porco at 2,159 metres. The ridge swings right to the southeast and the path has to contour round a number of difficult rock passages before reaching the summit at 2,399 metres. The descent is made by the `ordinary route' (voie normale) of ascent from Vizzavona in common use during summer and generally referred to as the Spelancello path. It is frequently cairned and descends initially to the northeast before swinging slightly south of east. From a small grassy plateau a steep and rocky couloir leads down to the ruined Bergeries de Puzzatelli at 1,500 metres, and from there the route continues by a forest path to Vizzavona railway station. Note carefully the PNR standard signs on the various footpaths around Vizzavona, since there are a number of alternatives at path junctions.

From the junction Monte d'Oro west the GR20 continues down into the upper basin of the

**2,000m**
*(Map ref H)*

**2:15**

Agnone, an awkward rocky negotiation of slabs and ribs down to about 1,620 metres. The basin flattens out into a plateau step and the path becomes once more obstructed by incipient maquis undergrowth. A further descent leads back to the left bank of the stream and the path, at about 1,490 metres, passes the ruins of the old refuge. It then crosses a small bridge on to the right bank of the stream down to the upper levels of the Cascades des Anglais.

**Cascades des Anglais**
*1,150m*

The Cascades provide a passage of great beauty with Corsican pine forest scattered among braided torrents and impressive cateracts which provides scores of perfect bathing spots. The route, sometimes traversing vast glaciated slabs to give open views of Monte d'Oro, keeps to the right bank until reaching a small suspension bridge, which is crossed. If the bridge is closed the crossing may require some easy boulder hopping.

**Detour,** *1 hr*
**COL DE VIZZAVONA**
✕
*1,163m*

**1:00**

**Detour** see left. Shortly before reaching the suspension bridge a waymarked path turns to the right and gives direct access, over an open shoulder with a ruined tower, to the Col de Vizzavona, the highest point on the N193.

From the river crossing at the suspension bridge the path diverges from the left bank and soon becomes a wide forestry road which leads to the N193 at the Maison Forestière de Vizzavona. Shortly before crossing the stream over a forestry bridge, there is a forestry road to the left, signposted to `Spelloncello'. This track eventually connects with the bottom of the `ordinary route' from Vizzavona to the summit of Monte d'Oro, already described, but also provides an alternative access to Vizzavona-Gare by making an alternative stream crossing to the north and entering Vizzavona close to the railway tunnel arch.

**Maison Forestière de Vizzavona**
*990m*
**Detour,** *15mins*
**VIZZAVONA-GARE**
🏠 ⛺ 🎣 ✕ 🍷 🚉 🚌
🚐

**Detour** see left. A narrow path on the hairpin bend, opposite the Maison Forestière, leads down to a lower hairpin on a minor road, past the Hotel Moderne, to the railway station. To

**2:45**

*920m*

*Vizzavona is in a significant position within the length of the GR20. It is approximately half way and very positively divides the arduous northern section from the less rigorous south. It is thus a convenient access point, not only for the easy lines of communication by train and road, but also as a place for those walkers not engaged upon the entire route to start or finish their chosen section.*

regain the GR20 from Vizzavona-Gare follow the road past the Hotel Moderne and after the first hairpin bend, by an open sided chapel-shrine turn right up a track through the forest which very soon reaches the N193 road. Turn left for a few yards to a wide forestry road on the right from which the GR, an old, well maintained mule track, diverges to the left after a few minutes. From pine forest, it rises through beech woods on long, well-graded hairpin loops. Water is available from a stream in the beech woods and after about 600 meters comes to well grazed open slopes. There are multiple animal tracks here and in bad visibility the waymarks should be followed carefully in a general northeasterly direction to the Bocca Palmente, a very shallow depression with a rocky outcrop on the left.

From the Maison Forestière a short road walk down the N193 gives direct access to the GR20 continuation towards the Bocca Palmente.

**BOCCA PALMENTE**
*1,640m*

The path crosses the col and descends, turning right, through the Bergeries d'Alzeta at 1,560 metres where a stream provides a water supply. The path then bears south and traverses the long eastern slope of the Renoso massif, crossing the gully of each successive stream and climbing around each projecting spur at a height between 1,350 and 1,600 metres. There are fallen trees and, in early season, streams to negotiate. The GR crosses a spur above the Bergeries/Cardo at 1,500 metres and then a little beyond the Bergeries de Scarpaccedie after a swift turn to the right, it climbs steeply through a beech wood to the ski road extension at a hairpin bend. Do not take the road ascending to the ski station hotel-restaurant, but take the lower alternative which descends very gradually towards the bar-restaurant and the adjacent older Refuge de Capanelle.

**2:30**

**REFUGE DE CAPANELLE**
⌂ Å ✕ ⏚
*1,586m*
*(Map ref I)*

**Alternative** route from the Refuge de Capanelle to the Plateau de Gialgone, at 1,591 metres, via the summit of Monte Renoso, 2,352 metres. Total time approximately 6 hours.

**Warning** Do not take this route in bad or even

*The summit of Renoso considered the finest viewpoint in the island; the view, best seen in the early morning, extends north to the Cinto massif, south of the southern extremity of the island, and west to Propriano.*

**6:00**

### REFUGE DE CAPANELLE
⌂ Å ✗ 🪑
*1,586m*

**2:50**

### Plateau de Gialgone
*1,591m*

**1:30**

threatening weather. It is not waymarked except by occasional cairns.

Follow the slopes to the top of the ski lift and ascend to the west over rough open ground. On reaching the north-south ridge line, the main island watershed, at about 2,000 metres, turn south on the large, stony plateau and follow the ridge line to the summit of Monte Renoso. The time taken for the ascent is 2 hours 50 minutes approximately. From the summit follow the true ridge south, narrow in places, to the Punta Orlandino, 2,273 metres, then descend southwest by way of a large stony couloir, dropping into the hollow of the highest of the 'pozzines'. The 'pozzines' descend in three tiered hollows, interlaced with streamlets, and are considered to be the finest examples in Corsica. From the lowest tier, at 1,783 metres, follow the main drainage stream southeast to the Bergeries des Pozzi, 1,746 metres. An old faint track contours to the east until, reaching the edge of the beech forest, it rejoins the main GR20 on the Plateau de Gialgone.

From Capanelle the GR20 follows the lower eastern spurs and gulleys of Monte Renoso. After passing the Bergeries de Traggette, the path makes a long descent down the left bank of the Ravine de Casso which it crosses by a bridge on the D169 ski road to the Refuge de Capanelle. Immediately afterwards it climbs away to the south, passing through pine, alder and scattered beech forest as it ascends gradually to the Plateau de Gialgone.

Amongst scattered beech trees the GR descends towards the south into the valley of the Marmano. The path, in some disrepair, follows several hairpin bends before it passes into the giant pines that cover the lower sides of the valley. Cross the torrent to the true right bank at 1,390 metres by means of large boulders or fallen trees. There is no bridge, and early in the season, during maximum snow melt, the crossing could be troublesome. The pines in this area are some of the tallest to be seen on the GR20 but a considerable number have fallen, some very awkwardly across the line of march.

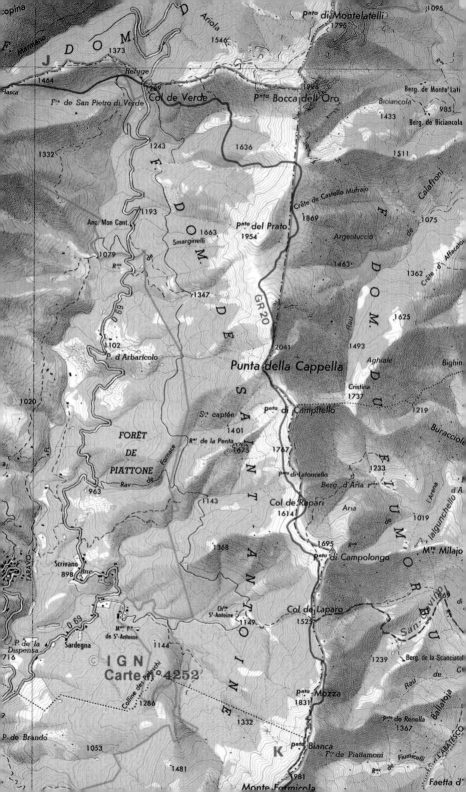

The path turns east, diverging from the stream as it climbs diagonally to the ridge line above at the small Col de la Flasca at 1,430 metres on the island's main watershed. A gradual descent from the wooded ridge down the south side leads to a forestry road to the Col de Verde.

### COL DE VERDE
△ Ⓐ ⓨ 🏛

*1,289m*
*(Map ref J)*

**1:15**

**Alternative route** from the Col de Verde to the Col de Laparo avoiding the high ridge route from the Refuge de Prati. Total time approximately 4¹/₂ hours saving 1 hour compared with GR route. The path, which is not waymarked, takes an old forestry road and contours at about 1,200 metres west of the main watershed, until it reaches the Chapelle Saint Antoine, which is also connected by road to the nearby Maison Forestière and the main D69 road up the Taravo valley. From the Chapelle Sainte Antoine take the left hand path uphill to the east, ascending the true left bank of a stream until, at a confluence, it transfers to the other bank and through groves of small beech trees reaches the Col de Laparo.

### COL DE VERDE
△ Ⓐ ⓨ 🏛

*1,289m*

**2:30**

From the Col de Verde, crossing the D69, take the forestry road for 10 minutes to where the GR20 turns left and to the east, climbing fairly steeply through pine forests until a slight levelling through open glades brings Punta de l'Oro into view. The path, bending southeast, dips slightly to rise once more in hairpin bends through beech woods to reach a rock spur at 1,636 metres. It then climbs a large, rough couloir on the right from lower left to upper right as far as the main watershed at the Col de Prato, 1,840 metres, a shallow depression east of the Punta del Prato. It extends south as an open plateau with rocky outcrops. Easy walking to the south through low juniper bushes, and a gradual descent through alder scrub brings you to the Refuge de Prati.

### REFUGE DE PRATI
△ Ⓐ

*1,840m*
**Warning** *No water between Prati and Usciolu unless diversion is made to source*

The GR crosses the wide, gently sloping depression southwest of the Refuge de Prati to the northern slope of Punta della Capella joining the main watershed ridge line once more. From this point the path follows the true watershed of the island as far as the Bocca

*below Refuge San Gavino.*

**2:45**

Agnone. On reaching a large rocky eminence at 1,988 metres greater difficulties are avoided by traversing the eastern side below the crest, although the traverse itself is awkward enough to need the use of hands. Snow frequently lies in the rocky hollows on this face until late in the season. The summit of Capella (2,041m) is bypassed at almost 2,000metres from where the crossing of a wide grassy col leads to the Punta di Campitello and its southern continuation, the Punta di Latoncellu. It reverts to the west side of the ridge proper by way of a small brèche and reaches a fairly exposed stretch involving some steep and occasionally awkward descents among large rocks, and with a spectacular view down into the Taravo valley. The route, passing a memorial plaque to a walker killed there in 1983, then reaches easier ground on the broad grassy Col de Rapari at 1,614 metres. Above the col on the eastern slope is a small beech wood. Above the wood the path contours easily on the west side of the Punta Campolongo from where, descending amongst stunted beech trees it reaches the Col de Laparo.

## Col de Laparo

*1,525m*
*Camping not allowed*
*The Low Level Alternative route from the Col de Verde and the Chapelle Saint Antoine joins the GR20 at the intersection with Walk 4, Catastajo to Cozzano stage.*

**Detour,** *3 hrs 30 mins*
**COZZANO**
⌂ ⍟ ⚒
*727m*
*5 hrs return*

**Detour** see left. Take the path to the right to Chapelle Saint Antoine. This path is on the Low Level alternative Col de Verde to Col de Laparo route already described and which turns sharply right to Col de Verde at Chapelle Saint Antoine. The path to Cozzano continues on at this junction and is fully described in Walk 4 Catastajo to Cozzano stage.

**Detour,** *15 mins*
**REFUGE SAN GAVINO**
⌂
*Water Source 5 mins below refuge*

**Detour** see left. The route follows the GR20 to the south on the east side of the ridge line and shortly below the Col de Laparo where the GR turns right the route branches left, to the east, marked with yellow flashes. The descent down

*2 hrs 30 mins*
**SAN GAVINO**
⌂ 🍷 ⚒
*460m*
*4 hrs return*

**2:00**

to the village of San Gavino continues on.

Standard Park signboards indicate the various paths available. South of the Col de Laparo follow the red and white markings of the GR20 carefully, avoiding the yellow waymarks of the alternative routes. At the junction on the path to the Refuge San Gavino the GR20, an ancient mule track, branches right to climb steeply up the eastern face of the Punta Mozza. It winds through a beechwood, avoiding rock butresses, descending and re-ascending around projecting spurs, until, finally, in a succession of hairpin bends it reaches a small brèche on the Col de Punta Mozza a ridge north of Formicola, at 1,800 metres, with a magnificent view to the north. Continuing on the west side of the pinnacled ridge the path climbs to the south, obstructed by dwarf alder but alternating with slabby schist covered in fine granules like small ball bearings underfoot. The steady ascent continues for about 1 kilometre to the Col du Brouillard, broad and slab-paved, at the northern end of Monte Formicola.

*(Map ref K)*

**Col du Brouillard**
*1,950m*

**1:10**

The GR crosses to the eastern slope of the col where it turns south once more, leaving the mule-track for an undulating path, contouring east of the Formicola summit. It eventually descends southwest to a small hanging cirque and the Refuge d'Usciolu.

**REFUGE D'USCIOLU**
⌂ ⛺

*1,750m*
*Splendid prospect to south and east, across the tributaries of the L'Arinella which flows east and becomes the river Travo. Beyond this, the landscape, highly unusual in Corsica, extends as an undulating plateau dissected by small streams, around the northwestern*

**0:10**

From the Refuge d'Usciolu a rough path ascends diagonally back to the main watershed ridge at the Col d'Usciolu.

*slopes of Monte Incudine, the only actual mountain summit crossed by the GR20.*

## Col d'Usciolu
*1,780m*
**Detour,** *2 hrs 30 mins*
**COZZANO**
⌂ ☍ ⚒
*727m*
*4 hrs return*

1:20

**Detour** see left. Follow the path with yellow markings descending to the west.

From the Col d'Usciolu the GR follows the main ridge southwest at an average height of 1,800 metres remaining on the true crest except where a succession of bizarrely shaped rock pinnacles bar the way. These have caused this difficult passage of steep ascents and descents to be baptised the `Arête des Statues'.

## `Arête des Statues'
*1,836m*

The GR descends, bypassing further pinnacles, before climbing once more to a deep brèche and going round the last of the rocks where an eroded track descends steeply through maquis to a grove of dwarf beech trees in a small hollow at 1,680 metres.

1:30

Note. This hollow is incorrectly marked on the IGN map as Bocca di Agnoni, a name more correctly applied to a broad flat col further south. The FFRP Topo-Guide has renamed this subsidiary depression the `Col de Monte Occhiato'. The Didier & Richard map, 1/50,000, Corse Sud, indicates the Bocca di Agnoni correctly.

A brief descent, to the south, down wooded slopes leads to the broad open depression, southwest of Monte Occhiato, properly named the Bocca di Agnone.

## Bocca di Agnone
*1,750m*
*Water source under beech trees at head of small stream.*
**Detour,** *2 hrs*
**ZICAVO**
⌂ ⌂ ✕ ☎
*700m*
*4 hrs return*

**Detour** see left. A path on the right descends to the southwest and then to the northwest contouring around Monte Occhiatu to Zicavo.

The GR20, initially turning east through magnificent beech forest turns to the south

**2:10**

*This is an ancient glaciated area with old moraines, now smooth and rounded, covered with beech woods. There are also many wandering pig herds that have torn up the ground in all directions.*

### Ruisseau de Casamintellu
**0:40**
*1,434m*
*Shed supplying drinks.*

### Old Refuge de Pedinielli
*1,623m*
*(Map ref L)*

**2:15**

### Monte Incudine
*2,134m*
*A cross marks the summit. The vertical crags of the southeast face above a steep, rocky couloir contrast strongly with the gentler aspect of the summit dome from the west. A semi-detached tower of large blocks is home to a flock of noisy alpine choughs. And as you look across the void*

**1:30**

again, descending through woods to a more open area and, eventually, to a wide depression with several small streamlets crossing it. There are a number of old tracks in this area and it is important to follow the GR waymarks. The path crosses a stretch of open heath with streams, to a junction from where a minor track, signposted with blue flashes on rocks, leads to the nearby Cavallara bergerie which may provide cheese, other snacks, and some rough accommodation if required. The GR climbs the shoulder directly south and descends to the left bank of the Casamintella river, crossing a cart track also signposted to the Cavallara bergerie. Slightly upstream is the footbridge over the river.

From the footbridge the GR20 ascends in well graded hairpin bends through beech woods to the edge of a small plateau and the ruins of the Refuge de Pedinielli.

From the site of the refuge the GR climbs directly uphill to the east through another beech grove at the top of which there is a piped water source. A steady ascent, first to the northeast and then directly east, across open terrain, brings you on to the north ridge of Monte Incudine at the Col de Luana, 1,805 metres, where the route turns sharply right to the south. Climb the ridge to a notch behind a small rock pinnacle where there is a fine view of the craggy summit of Punta di Tintennaja, 2,018 metres high, and again, to the right, taking a long curving line east of the ridge proper to the easily surmounted summit of Monte Incudine.

The route follows the ridge southwest as far as a small gap called the Col des Forgerons at 2,025 metres from where the descent towards Asinao begins. The upper part is steep and the waymarked route traces a line of weakness across slabs and down small gullies and grooves choked with loose rock. The red and white flashes meander about the upper levels of the couloir, occasionally even re-ascending to avoid particular difficulties.

**Warning** It is important, particularly in conditions of poor visibility to follow the waymarks since

*of the Asinao ravine, the toothed ridges of the Bavella region are a compelling feature to the southeast.*

it is easy, even tempting at times, to follow an apparently easier alternative only to end up on dangerously steep terrain.

Awkward passages become fewer and the track straightens towards the bottom of the couloir where you descend more gently through spiky berberis, bright yellow in late June, to the Refuge de'Asinao.

## REFUGE D'ASINAO
△ Å

*1,536m*
*The Bergeries d'Asinao where camping is allowed can be reached direct from the refuge.*
**Detour,** *3 hrs 30 mins*

## QUENZA
Ⓗ ⍓

*813m*
*4 hrs return*

From the refuge the path descends, roughly southwest, towards the spring known as the Fontaine de Partusu. From a junction the GR goes to the left and descends further through scattered pines to the stream bed of the Ruisseau d'Asinao.

**Detour** see left. From the junction a path goes to the right, following the right bank of the stream south southwest to Quenza.

## Ruisseau d'Asinao
*1,340m*

The GR crosses the stream on large boulders to the left bank, and following an old forestry track along the stream, after an initial rise, continues more or less on the same contour through a pine forest. About 4 kilometres from the stream you come to a junction signposted `Variante Alpinisme, Col de Bavella, 4 hrs'.

## Junction
*1,300m*
*The High Level alternative route leaves the GR20.*

**Alternative route.** High level variation through the Bavella Towers waymarked with double yellow flashes.

**Warning** This route includes one fairly exposed passage on steep rock, assisted by a fixed handrail. Other sections require considerable care since a slip would have serious consequences. The route should not be attempted in bad or threatening weather.

From the junction a very steep path, with minimal hairpin bends climbs up towards the Towers of Asinao. Eventually rising above the trees, the path climbs diagonally to the right across open ground to the Col de Pargulu at 1,662 metres, one of the finest viewpoints in the entire length of the GR20 overlooking the perpendicular confusion of the crags and pinnacles to the northeast.

0:30

0:50

2:30

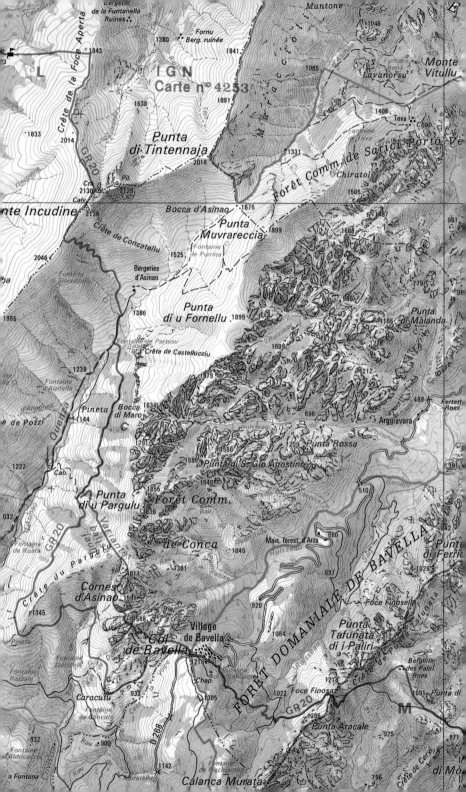

From the Col de Pargulu the route traces a winding path through a group of rock towers immediately to the south. At first descending to a narrow traverse on the side of a precipitous hollow, the way is interrupted by an undercut steep slab protected by a fixed cable, from where, with characteristic contortions, the route eventually climbs to a deep brèche. A steepish gully leads down from the brèche, requiring care due to loose boulders and vegetation. Lower down the path turns left to easier ground and, by a descending traverse, enters a pine forest. It crosses a minor depression before rising on to open space at the Col de Bavella.

**Junction**

**3:00**

The GR20 continues through forest following the contours until it comes out into the open on a prominent shoulder at 1,200 metres which overlooks the entire Criviscia basin. This shoulder is part of the ridge that descends from the Col de Pargulu. Still contouring, the path turns northeast, with splendid views of the Bavella pinnacles, and continues in this way, penetrating each gully to reach its lowest point at the Donicelli stream, from where it follows on an arc back to the southeast. Rocky embrasures coming down from the pinnacles above are easily negotiated round a final corner and the path, once more in a northeasterly direction ascends across forested slopes to the large open area at the Col de Bavella, marked by a shining white statue of the madonna - Notre Dame de la Neige.

**COL DE BAVELLA**
△ ▲ ✕ ⌒

*1,218m*
*The summer village of Bavella below the col to the east is now a tourist centre.*
**Detour**
**ZONZA**
**1:20**
⌂ ✕ ⌒ ▭

*Follow the D268 road from the village of Bavella for 9 kilometres.*

The GR leaves the village from the bend of the top hairpin on the D268 road, adjacent to the higher bar restaurant, and follows a wide forestry road towards the southeast. It soon turns left, descending through trees to another wide forest track and crosses the Saint Pierre stream at a small concrete dam at 1,000 metres. On the right bank the path once more leaves the forest road, ascending slightly north of east on a gradual line towards the ridge. The path, passing through young pine trees turns up more sharply towards the ridge and steepens before crossing it on a well defined little notch called Foce Finosa. South of this crossing the GR20 never again reaches 1,200 metres and there is a real sense of descending at last towards the eastern seaboard.

## Foce Finosa

*1,206m*

*There is a splendid view of the Buvone chain of summits, from the Punta di Bonifaccio, on the left, to the Col de Fumigosa at the head of the Ravin d'Aracale. Closer, on the extreme right, it is just possible to see the Campanile de Saint-Lucie, a giant finger of rock, looking grotesquely unstable to the eye.*

**0:45**

The GR20 descends from the col by an old path in steep hairpin bends through forested crags until, at about 1,000 metres, it turns left to contour below the steepest ground. At a rather faint junction the path diverges to the left, rising in a gentle curve towards the col below the southeast face of the Punta Tafunata di i Paliri. The Refuge de Paliri is close by the ruined bergeries.

## REFUGE DE PALIRI

⌂ Å

*1,060m*

*(Map ref M)*

*There is a water source on the path about 200 metres from the refuge in the direction of Bavella. A better supply is available about 200 metres below the refuge.*

**2:00**

From the refuge the GR descends to the south shortly rejoining the old path to Conca. Through beautiful pine forest the path passes southwest, to the right, of the Punta di i Paliri and rises slightly to the Bocca Bracciutu at 971 metres from where there is a fine open view to the northeast. Climbing to a broad col on the northern spur of Punta di Monte Sordu, the path, turns south on to the eastern slope, losing height once more. Over this section the path is frequently invaded by maquis and the point at which one turns right, steeply uphill, is not too obvious. A steep little climb over a very eroded track takes you to a fairly broad col, the brèche de Villaghello at 1,040 metres. More open terrain with only scattered pines set among low bouldery ridges and large slabs follows.

**Warning** The waymarked path across this undulating plateau should be followed carefully. In poor visibility it would be easy to stray off course among the maquis fringed rocky hollows.

From the southern edge of this unusual terrain the path swings to the left, almost due east, and descends through fire damaged forest to the ruined Bergeries de Capellu.

## Bergeries de Capellu

*850m*

*Water source 200 metres to the north on old access path from Solenzara region.*

The GR follows the ancient access path to the south, descending progressively through deep maquis that now covers this fire damaged area. On a sudden loop, the path turns east before crossing a small stream among a surviving grove of pines in the Ravine de Punta Pinzuta.

2:00

**Bocca d'Usciolu**
*587m*

0:40

**CONCA**
*252m*

The path follows the left bank to the south and, on reaching a large rock outcrop, descends through hairpin bends to the right recrossing the stream where there is a small waterfall and a pool. From the stream the GR climbs the true right side of the ravine to a notch in the ridge above, and the long contouring path, high above the Casale stream, stretches into the distance. Unfortunately this entire area has been devasted by fire and the long open traverse of the hillside towards the last ridge crossing is rather tedious, and totally without shade. The narrow cleft between tall rocks which marks the Bocca d'Usciolu, the final ridge crossing, is happily more appropriate to the last stage of a great walk.

The descent from the gap is fairly steep and the path, through deep undergrowth, is very eroded. The pink roofs of Conca and the Mediterranean coastline are in constant view and although both offer relief of a kind the ancient Fontaine de Radicale to be found in a cool glade, shortly before joining the metalled road may be even more refreshing. This is cork oak country and their blackened boles, typical of this hot, southeastern corner of the island, accompany you downhill to the smart little houses and well kept gardens of Conca.

# WALK 2

## Between Sea and Mountain: Calenzana - Cargese

This very beautiful footpath crosses an area recently described as one of the very few `Natural Sites of World Interest' (UNESCO, 1983). Close to the finest peaks and mountain massifs and overlooking creeks, capes, and wild sea depths, it combines leisure with the exploration of natural settings and provides exercise but no great difficulty, with occasional opportunities for sea or river bathing.

The recommended walking seasons are Spring, from Easter onwards; autumn, until Christmas; summer, if you like the heat, but take care to avoid heat-stroke; wear a hat, and in summer set out early in the day. The route is fully arrowed and waymarked in orange.

## Information and Suggestions

*Hostels in the Nature Park:* The hostels are more comfortable than the traditional refuges. They have beds with mattress and bedding, as well as showers, wc, heating. Self-catering facilities are available (gas and equipment), but you may also order meals in most hostels. Note: the accommodation in Revinda (E Case) is very basic (no booking), and is outside the village. It has cooking facilities, and bedding. A booking system is being planned. Telephone the hostel wardens, preferably at meal-times or in the evening; the wardens are country people who work on the land.

*Water:* Check supplies before setting out, and refill when passing springs noted on the map, particularly in summer.

*Forest Fires:* Always take care, never under-estimate the potential speed of a fire; remember that smoke can incapacitate people ahead of the flames, with the risk of asphyxiation.

**CALENZANA**

255m
Mountain Information
Centre

5:00

To reach the departure point, which is also that of the GR20, from the hostel on the way into Calenzana, go through to the southwest edge of the village, and at 300 metres take the good mule track up towards the Ortiventi spring, 540 metres. About 100 metres beyond the spring you leave the route shared with the GR20 and fork right, westwards towards the broad col of Bocca a u Corsu, 581 metres, with a very fine view over Calenzana and the Balagna villages. The path then follows the old `Postman's Track' down past a beautiful public spring, and beyond the Sambuccu stream joins the ONF track at 412 meters, close to a small spring. The route curves round on the level through the completely replanted Sambuccu woods, crosses a small col at 454 metres, then descends gently to the bridge over the Ficarella at 360 metres. Beyond the bridge the footpath follows the river bank, and after a short climb through hairpin bends

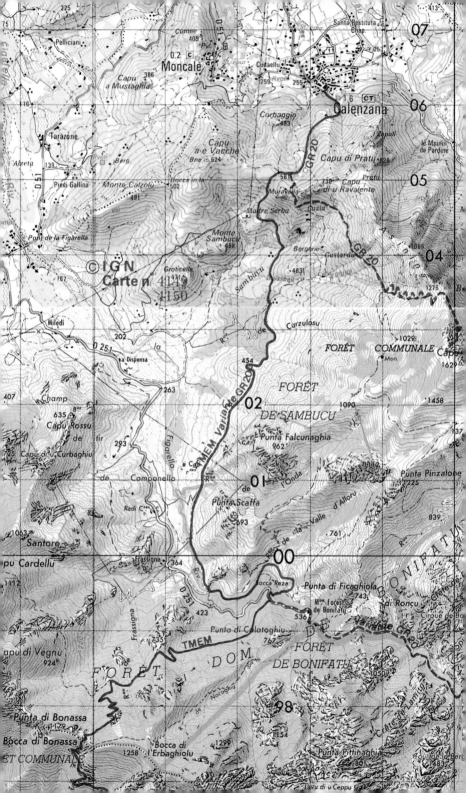

### `Santa Restituda` - St. Restitude - Calenzana

1.5km approx. northeast of Calenzana on the D151, the chapel of St. Restitude guards the relics of the village's patron saint and the companions of her martyrdom, celebrated with fervour on 21 May. The crypt contains a magnificent marble tomb, discovered by archaeologists in 1951, together with a 12th century fresco depicting the martyrdom of St. Restitude and her companions early 4th century, with Calvi shown in the background.

meets the D251 road at Bocca Reza, at 510 metres, 1 kilometre below the Maison Forestière at Bonifatu and the forest inn.

**BONIFATU**

Take the D51 down to Boca Reza, and turn off left along the circular forest track, climbing gently up to the southwest through Laricio or maritime pines and ilex to a height of 830 metres. Here the path turns south off the track and climbs swiftly through hairpin bends under the pines. At 1,120 metres the path reaches the Bonassa spring, just below the Bonassa col, and then the col itself, at 1,153 metres. The path slopes down to the south through a pine wood and then becomes almost horizontal, curving round the valley like a circular forest track, crosses several streams, still in the forest, and drops down to Bocca di Lucca at 589 metres. From there a very good footpath crosses to the west slope of Capu Brugatiu, runs along to a small col and over to the south slope above the Prunicciale sheep-pens, finally reaching the hamlet of Tuvarelli, at 100 metres.

7:00

**TUVARELLI**

*100m*

Take the dirt track to the left, at 100 metres, heading west and then northwest along the right bank of the river Fango. Between low walls and well-maintained fields. It follows the old Calvi - Niolu transhumance track through juniper and myrtle bushes along a very attractive route to reach Ponte Vecchiu, 46 metres with a fine view of the great dam and the Paglia Orba, 2,325 metres. Continue along a good dirt track, first by the river and then moving away from it, and climb gently up to the agricultural estate of La Vaitella - Guaitella on IGN map, 65 metres. From the farm buildings, follow the fine avenue of trees to the D51 road at the entrance to Vaitella campsite.

4:15

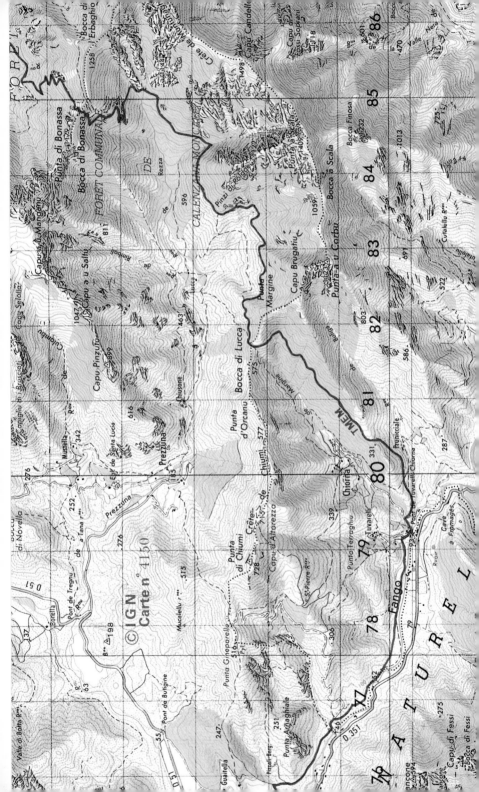

**`Sa Santa Di U Niolu'**
Legend tells that some hundreds of years ago, following the destruction of a monastery - was it Girulatu? A Setra? Santa Maria? - several other monasteries wished to provide a home for its miraculous statue of the Virgin and Child. To settle the argument, the statue was strapped to a mule's saddle: wherever the animal finally stopped, the Virgin would be worshipped. The mule wandered for two days, then stopped at Casamaccioli. Since then Corsica's greatest pilgrimage takes place there every 7, 8 and 9 September, with its famous winding `harvest' procession; combined since 1835 with the island's most important rural fair.

**VAITELLA OR GUAITELLA**
⚐ ⛩
*38m*
*Watersports, diving club.*

Turn left along the D51 for 600 metres; on reaching the D81 turn left across the five-span bridge - designed by Eiffel - then turn right along the D351 Galeria road for about 800 metres, crossing a small bridge on a bend. Just beyond the bridge take the dirt track to the left up through the maquis. The dirt track soon becomes a footpath, climbs up to 170 metres, then continues west virtually along the contour line, with a very fine view over the mouth of the River Fango. A slight descent brings you to the village of Galeria at 40 metres.

**GALÉRIA**
🏠 ⌂ ⚐ ✕ ⚲ ⛩ ▭
*40m*

To pick up the footpath again follow the orange waymarking from the main street. It leaves Galeria from the highest part of the village, at 50 metres, by a track between walls, heading southwest along beside the River Tavulaghiu and then up the stream bed itself, veering from one side to the other as convenient. From the foot of Punta di u Lucciu, 152 metres, the path climbs up in a series of bends dominated at first by the red cliffs of the Capu Tondu, then gradually moves away and into a wood of ilex below the Lucciu ridge, with a very open view over Galeria and its gulf gradually appearing. It continues through the ilex up to the Lucciu ridge, 697 metres, and very soon you reach Punta di a Literniccia, 778 metres, overlooking the seaside village of Girolata. Follow the ridge along to the west, to an altitude marker at 720 metres, not indicated on the map, keeping close to the line of the crest which drops away steadily to the right, taking care not to veer away onto the western slopes. After reaching the 602 metres marker you begin the descent to Bocca

*5:30*

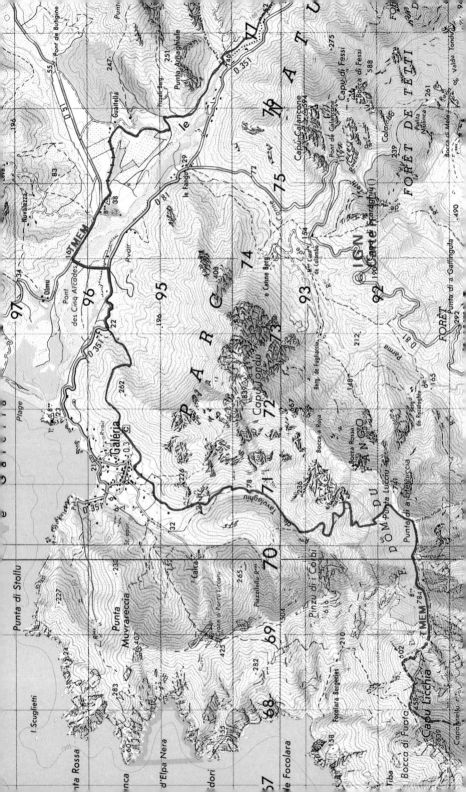

di Fuata, 458 metres. Follow a path that gently slopes down to the 315 metres marker, then leaves the ridge and runs down to reach Girolata along the shore.

**GIROLATA**

*36m*

From Girolata take the excellent footpath heading southeast to a small col overlooking the Cala di Tuara. Turn back left and carry on up, following the ridge and heading generally northeast, past the 267 metres marker, to reach the D81 road at 352 metres. Cross the road and continue northeast along the ridge to the Putna di u Munditoghiu. The path follows the ridge up eastwards, to the foot of the Punta di U Tartavellu, 825 metres. Bear round gradually to the south as far as a small col, and then full south up towards Punta Salisei, which you pass on your left, just before a public spring at 790 metres. Next, the footpath veers gently southwest, following the sometimes narrow and exposed ridge. Continue steadily and carefully along the ridge to the Capu di Curzu, 852 metres, with an outstanding view. From there you head west and then south down to the ruined Summatoghiu sheep-pens, and cross two side valleys by a series of tight hairpin bends to reach Curzu at 290 metres.

6:30

**CURZU**

The path sets out from the top of the village, heading southeast, climbs a little, and then follows the contour line above the bay of Caspiu and the village of Partinello, crosses an open shoulder and curves round the slope of Monte San Angelu facing the sea to Culetta at the top end of Partinello.

**Detour,** *1hr*
**PARTINELLO**

*281m*

**Detour** see left. Turn off right, down into the village of Partinello.

---

### The Osani Coal-field
The jagged cliffs of the Capu d'Osani consist of lava flows from the time of Monte Cintu's volcanic activity, in the late Primary Era. They conceal coal deposits, with several seams appearing at surface level in the Osani-Curzu area, particularly on the slope down to Curzu, slightly below the Licciola ridge. Mining continued until 1914 and the coal extracted (1,000 tonnes) was shipped away from the beach at Gradelle.

**3:00**

Return to Culetta and bear right along the path, down to the River Vetricella; cross it by the ford, which usually presents no problems, but in case of heavy rain, see the alternative route, below. From the ford, follow the footpath up the opposite slope to meet the track running from Serriera to Pinitu, an abandoned village 500 metres to the left at 250 metres, turn right along a formerly heavily used track, broad and easy, and at the shoulder known as Bocca a u Furcatu, 180 metres, turn left to reach Serriera, 120 metres. The hostel is 300 metres below the village on the road to Porto.

**Alternative route,** Partinello to Serriera Recommended when the rivers are very full, also at times of high fire risk in summer, or of persistent drought in autumn. From Culetta cross the top of Partinello to the cemetery. Take a dirt track which at first is suitable for vehicles, down the seaward mountain slope of Aghialitu. This used to be the main link between Serriera and Partinello, and despite recent road-works many remaining stretches can be followed along the lower section, in preference to the bulldozer's track. On reaching the D81 turn left to cross the Vetricella River by a road bridge at 50 metres, then 100 metres farther on take a footpath up to the left along a spur and at Bocca a u Furcatu fork right to Serriera.

**SERRIERA**
🏠 △ ✕ ⍭ ⚒
*120m*

Cross the footbridge over the Santa Marita stream, below Serriera, and follow the Lonca forest road for 2 kilometres. The path bends sharply right, at 268 metres where a broad cleared strip several dozen metres wide continues as a footpath heading up southwards

---

**Formation of the communes of Osani, Partinello and Serriera.**
Until 1862 the entire Sia territory formed part of the mountain commune of Evisa. The inhabitants divided their time between the `mountain' where they chiefly cultivated sweet chestnuts, and the `seaside', where they grew cereals. The population shifted with the livestock transhumance, and the local economy was thus based on the complementary exploitation of sea and mountain traditional throughout the island. Part of the population finally settled permanently in one place, and this sociological development was recognised in the creation of the three separate communes in 1862.

**6:15**

along a ridge to Capu San Petru. Follow this footpath, crossing the wall marking the edge of the state forest, and after a steep stretch reach a rocky viewpoint at 700 metres overlooking Serriera and the country round. Continue up to reach the summit ridge, 900 metres, by way of a chestnut wood. Head westwards out of the woodland, with its many centenarian junipers, to reach Capu San Petru itself at 914 metres, with an impressive view over Porto. Go down the same way to the chestnut woods, and follow the path eastwards through a pine wood with heather undergrowth interspersed with chestnuts. After passing a small building - a chestnut drier at Pedua, you fork right to begin the long descent southwestwards down the Vitrone ravine. The path leads down between imposing walls of red porphyry, and follows the bed of the stream in a series of clear and well designed hairpin bends. On leaving the ravine the path veers south, then east, following the contour line across a series of ridges until it reaches Ota at 320 metres.

**OTA**
*320m*

From the school buildings the footpath goes gently downhill, shaded by olive trees. This old and much frequented track is still broad and much of it is paved. Cross the River Porto by the now restored Ponte Vecchiu at 200 metres, a `genoese' bridge remarkable for its height and the delicacy of its lines. Carry on between the road and the river for 250 metres, to the confluence of the Lonca and Aïtone rivers, where you cross the road, and the path enters the Spelunca gorge on the left bank of the Aïtone. In the shade of very varied vegetation it follows the course of the river bed gently up to the confluence of the Aïtone and the Tavulella

**2:55**

---

**The Legend of Capu d'Ota**

Dominating the village of Ota, the rock of Capu d'Ota appears to threaten the houses. Inquiring visitors often ask villagers if they feel safe with this monstrous stone block poised above their heads. To which `paesani' serenely reply that monks have always held up the rock with heavy chains, so there is absolutely no cause for alarm. Divine grace, confidence in good fortune, or simply rural humour delighting in visitors' credulity? Whatever the truth, people sleep peacefully at night in Ota.

and crosses the Tavulella by the `genoese' Zaglia bridge at 280 metres. The footpath continues through very steep but regular hairpin bends, climbing quickly with frequent retaining walls, along the rocky cliff above the Zaglia bridge, to a spring at 510 metres and on under cover of ilex which gradually give way to maritime pines. Although less steep here the path still climbs steadily, and as it does so the view opens out with a magnificent panorama down over the gorges of Spelunca and Gulf of Porto. The path reaches Evisa beside the cemetery at 800 metres. Follow the road to the village centre at 850 metres.

**EVISA**

⌂ 🛆 🍷 ⚓

*85m*

1:30

From the Post Office pick up the tarmac road at the bottom of the village; turn left along it for 300 metres, then right, on to a footpath leading down to the Tavulella river. Cross the river by a cable footbridge to the abandoned hamlet of `U Tassu' at 730 metres where you turn sharp right, westwards, through the chestnut trees. The view quickly opens out as the path continues above the road bridge across the Tavulella, and along the contour line to the village of Marignana at 730 metres.

**MARIGNANA**

⌂

*720m*

Climb up from the refuge, 730 metres, through the village of Marignana to reach Bocca au Mamucciu, above the municipal sports-ground at 824 metres. Bear right, west, along the ridge from the col, then southwest along the contour line above the Fiuminale valley. Beyond several stretches of chestnut trees there is a remarkable viewpoint at 920 metres looking down this valley to the point where it meets the sea at Sagone.

---

### `Minicale', Corsican Poet

Born in Evisa in 1868, Minicale died there in 1963, but he was known throughout Corsica, and belonged to a generation rich in poets, essayists and story-tellers who used the Corsican language. In particular he made use of the poetic form known as `Chjami et rispondi' - questions and answers, a sort of word game in which, sometimes for hours at a time, two poets would exchange improvisations to the rhythm of a traditional chant. Moving from one local fair to another, Minicale pursued his art with enthusiasm, improvising humourous allusions to blend into the ballad and delight his many listeners, who were, and still are enthusiastic follower of this style of poetry, which was the direct descendant of the oldest Mediterranean traditions.

**6:30**

Continue along an excellent footpath overlooking the whole of the valley, past a public spring at 940 metres to `Culetta a u Prunu' at 970 metres - another viewpoint. Next, turn downhill to the Vaccareccia stream, 780 metres before heading uphill again on a long open climb, with further very fine views over Sagone to Bocca Acquaviva at 1,102 metres where there is a public spring a few dozen metres below, on the western slope. Follow the route from the col to a viewpoint at the Casta sheep-pens, then down to Revinda, fairly steeply at first, before plunging into the shade of the tall and beautiful maquis of the Rognia valley. The footpath continues through the shade of ilex, arbutus and heather, the slope gradually becoming less severe, and passes semi-circular platforms with retaining walls, the relics of former charcoal-burning here, and on the other side of the river, a disused coppermine at 580 metres. From this point the route gradually moves away from the main river-bed, without much altitude, to a turning at 560 metres. The footpath to the right leads to Revinda, 535 metres, the one on the left carries on to the hamlet of E Case and the refuge, 605 metres.

**REVINDA/E CASE**

⌂

*605m*

From E Case head south, and after a few minutes on the level go down to the Mastica stream, then up again to Petracqua, a plateau, partly covered with fine arbutus trees at 620 metres, overlooking the Pianu Maggioe ridge. The footpath continues along the open ridge, with a panoramic view over the Gulf of Chiumi between the Pointe d'Omigna and the Pointe d'Orchinu, to reach an altitude of 570 metres where it turns sharply to the left, close to a small rocky spur. The path down to the Esigna

---

**Desertification**

Scarcely fifty years ago the village of E Case had about 100 inhabitants, including more than twenty children, and a school. The last inhabitant, who left the village in 1947, lived in the house now restored by the Regional Nature Park as a refuge. Fifteen minutes' walk away, opposite, the hamlet of Revinda hs six permanent inhabitants - fewer than the number of dead whose names appear on the war memorial. Symptomatic of the circumstances affecting the whole interior of the island, this demographic outflow explains the deep malaise suffered by Corsica in modern times.

**2.50**

valley is very steep, particularly the first stretch, through fairly sparse maquis of cistus and arbutus. Gradually the slope becomes gentler, though still quite stiff, and you reach the ruined sheep-pens of Santa Lucia at 220 metres. In front of the sheep-pens the footpath crosses a hillock covered with aromatic nepeta, a local species of wild marjoram. 800 metres farther on the footpath crosses the Esigna stream at 150 metres, and continues along the left bank to the stream, in the shade of the immense oaks of the Esigna woods, and crosses the stream again by a thick growth of myrtle bushes, to reach the village of Lozzi at 50 metres. On leaving the village head directly south and climb the facing slope to a col at 380 metres overlooking Cargese. From there turn west along an old heavily-used path between walls, to Cargese, at the end of the route.

**CARGESE**
🏠 ⌂ ⚑ ✕ 🄳
*96m*

---

**The Corsica Regional Nature Park**

Extending across the watershed ridge dividing the `far-side' mountains (u Pumonte) from the `near-side' over (u Cismonte), the Corsica Regional Nature Park covers 82 communes. The mountains are its chosen domain, for the Park includes all the main mountain massifs of the island, and its seaward aspect, `the mountain reaching down to the sea', constitutes one of the jewels in Corsica's extraordinary varied heritage. Since its creation in 1971 the Park organisation has worked towards twin goals: to protect wild life of all kinds, and to share in a revival of the rural economy. The loss of population which has affected communities of the Corsican interior for decades is menacing the island's ecological balance, and the abandoned terrain is threatened by increasingly devastating fires. Renewal of the rural economy, however, also involves fighting to maintain a Corsican culture that is in harmony with its natural and historical environment. By encouraging pastoral activity and stimulating potential development in the most widely scattered communes, and by encouraging forms of tourism which are sympathetic both to the environment and to the people, the Park contributes to the protection of Corsica's essential values. In the spirit of this philosophy, we invite you to explore the `Strada tra Mare e Monti', while urging the greatest respect for wild life of all kinds as you walk and explore.

# WALK 3

This footpath, is generally practicable from mid-May to end of November; up-to-date information is available from the Nature Park. The path can be undertaken by anyone used to walking on moderate mountain routes. It is arrowed and waymarked in orange. Walkers are strongly recommended to set out from Sermano, which makes it possible to explore the magnificent Boziu region. To ensure the link onwards to Sermano the hostel wardens are prepared to collect walkers at Corte.

**SERMANO**
△
*760m*

4Km
0:50

**CASTELLARE-DI-MERCURIO**
△
*610m*

14Km
5:20

**CORTE**
🏠 △ 🛉
*420m*
*Regional Nature Park Information Centre open July - October.*

13Km
5:30

**SEGA**
△ 🛉
*1,190m*
*Open air swimming.*

Take the footpath from the middle of the village, near the post office, through the back lanes to the San Nicolao chapel. Following a fairly level walk the path dips down to the Castellare stream, 540 metres, and up again to the village of Castellare.

From the village a long climb leads to the San Martinu chapel, 904 metres. You then `plunge' down to the hamlet of Piedivaldo, 620 metres, and on to the hamlet of Poggiolu and the village of Santa Lucia, 820 metres. A gentle slope leads down to Bocca di Civenti, 785 metres. From this col an occasionally steep descent brings you to the Bistugliu stream, 384 metres, followed by a slight rise to a small col at 430 metres. Soon after, turn right along the CD14 road, to reach Corte in about ten minutes.

Set off from the access road to the Corte `Citadelle', about 250 metres to the north of the Citadelle (Park sign, altitude 454 metres). Follow a well-marked mule track steadily up the left bank of the River Tavignano, through a barren area which gradually changes to more or less full maquis coverage. Cross the Tavignano by a suspension footbridge, at 760 metres, and carry on up the right bank of the Tavignano, through a magnificent forest of Lariccio pines, with occasional short steep stretches. The path becomes more even on the final stretch, as it approaches the Sega refuge, at 1,190 metres, beside the Tavignano.

From the refuge take the footbridge across the Tavignano, and turn immediately right. After a very short slope down to the Mente stream the path climbs steeply to about 1,350 metres,

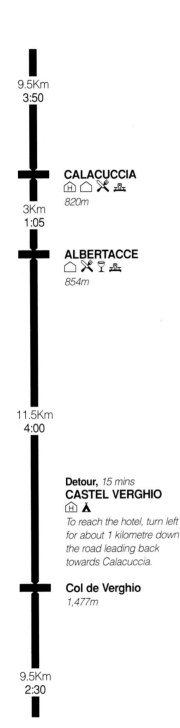

9.5Km
3:50

**CALACUCCIA**
🏠 △ ✕ 🕳
*820m*

3Km
1:05

**ALBERTACCE**
△ ✕ 🍸 🕳
*854m*

11.5Km
4:00

**Detour,** *15 mins*
**CASTEL VERGHIO**
🏠 ⚠
*To reach the hotel, turn left
for about 1 kilometre down
the road leading back
towards Calacuccia.*

**Col de Verghio**
*1,477m*

9.5Km
2:30

half way up the slope, then steadily on to the Bonaccie sheep-pens at 1,500 metres, crosses the forest track and reaches the highest point, Bocca a l'Arinella, at 1,592 metres. From here the path drops steadily, past the Casartine sheep-pens at 1,169 metres, to the Calacuccia dam, 794 metres, and into the village of Calacuccia.

Sidossi, 800 metres, on a track following the contour-line, then along beside the western end of the Calacuccia lake to the Mulinellu stream, 800 metres, and straight on to the village of Albertacce, 854 metres, at la Croix.

Take the path from Albertacce cross to the Muricciolu bridge by the Nature Park mill, 850 metres. Cross the Viru stream and follow the steep track up to the 1,115 metres altitude marker where a track leads off to Calasima. Continue along an almost horizontal footpath, crossing two streams, the Alzetto at 1,084 metres and the Castellu at 1,149 metres, and then the Vilnacce plateau, 1,190 metres. From here the track bears round to the San Rimeriu bridge, 1,049 metres, and across the Ciatterinu stream. Follow the forest track for 100 metres, then turn right; the path climbs steadily, passing near the Ciatterina Barracks, to the Col de Verghio, crossing the GR20 and the road twice along the way.

Return from the hotel to the Col de Verghio road. The departure point is behind the statue, 100 metres from the spring. Take the footpath down through hairpin bends to a small reservoir. Turn right on to a forest track to the Casterica bridge, and follow the path up for 100 metres; then turn left onto the footpath down to the Aïtone. Cross the `Scouts' bridge to reach the Aïtone holiday village; passing it on your left, and follow the path into the Lariccio pine forest,

**EVISA**

850m

coming out at a small barrage. Next you pass the Aïtone swimming area and some waterfalls to reach the D84 road. Turn along it for 100 metres, then take the footpath to the right, at the Evisa sign, passing through a plantation of magnificent chestnuts, to reach the village of Evisa.

For the 3 final stages of this walk: Evisa - Marignana - Revinda/E Case - Cargese, see the 3 last stages of Walk 2 (page 79), which follow the same route.

**Alternative Route** Sermano to Marignana This alternative route in nine separate stages enables walkers to explore several small regions in turn. The paths are entirely practicable from mid-May until November, but the route is not yet fully equipped; several stages still lack a hostel. If you wish to be among the first to use this new route, advance booking of overnight lodging is advisable; the local communes are usually very pleased to help. Further information is available fom the Nature Park.

Evisa

To reach Sermano, contact the hostel manager who will collect you from Corte. Taxis are also available.

**SERMANO**
640m

4:00

**POGGIO DI VENACO**
540m

4:00

**NOCETA**
540m

4:20

**CANAGLIA (VIVARIO)**
720m

2:40

**L'ONDA**
1,420m

3:50

**PASTRICCIOLA**
600m

4:30

**GUAGNO**
750m

4:00

**SOCCIA**
730m

6:30

**RENNO**
913m

3:00

**MARIGNANA**
715m

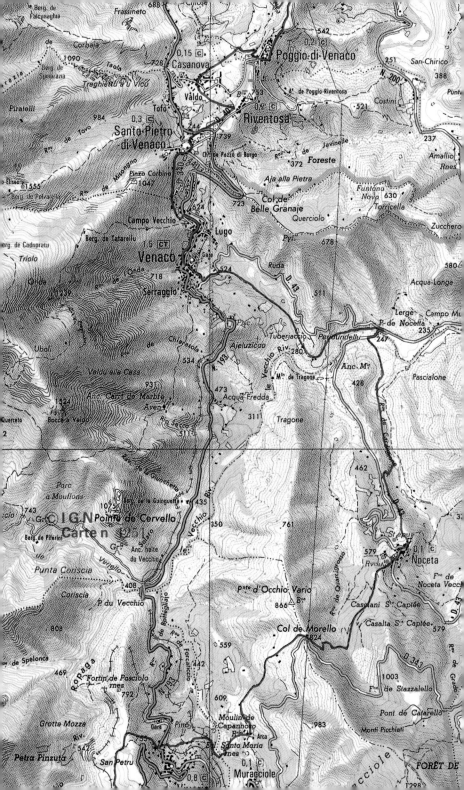

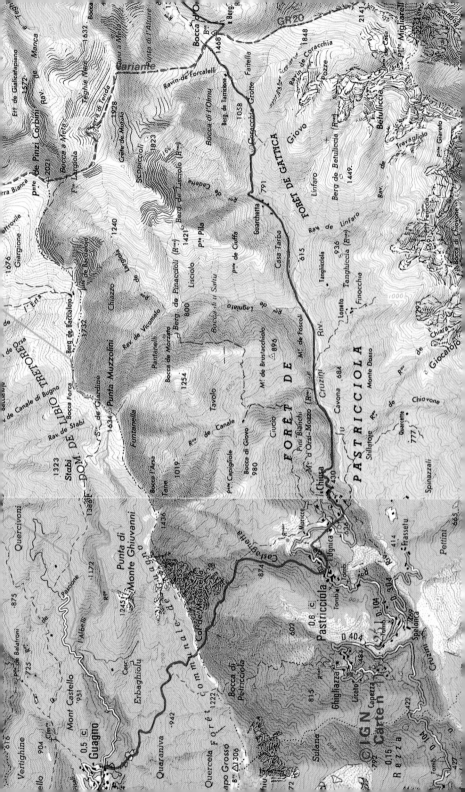

# WALK 4

This footpath is practicable from mid-May until November, and can be undertaken by anyone used to mountain walking at moderate altitudes. The route is fully waymarked in orange. It also provides access to the beautiful regions of Fiumorbu and Taravu.

## GHISONACCIA

*Approx. 15km by road to the start of the walk at Sualello.*

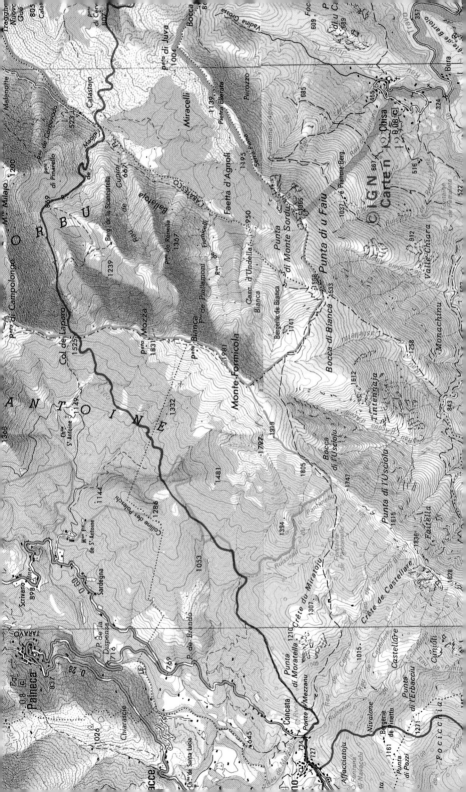

**Acquacitosa (Sualello)**
*69m*
*1.5km south on the road*
*from Abbazia Chalybeate*
*spring*

**1:00**

Turn west on to a minor road for about 150 metres to the starting point of the footpath. The track goes steadily up through the maquis and crosses the road twice to reach the village of Serra-di-Fiumorbu.

**SERRA-DI- FIUMORBU**
⌂ ♆ ⚒
*460m*

**3:30**

Take the Ventiseri road from the village, then turn right on to the footpath for 1 kilometre. A steady climb brings you to the highest point of this stage, 957 metres, almost beneath the summit of Quarcio Grosso. A continuous slope leads down to Bocca Minagoli, at 893 metres, and a short stretch across the hillside brings you to Bocca di Juva, at 866 metres. From here take the long slope down, heading first in the direction of the hamlet of Ania and then towards the Punta di Cervo, 807 metres, crossing the Abbatesco stream on the way, to reach Catastajo at the foot of the hill.

**CATASTAJO**
⌂
*523m*

Starting near the hostel and heading southwestwards at first, the footpath climbs steadily through a magnificent wood of maritime pines, then follows the Catastajo stream to a beech-wood leading up to the Col de Laparo, 1,525 metres, and a junction with the GR20.

**Junction,**
*the provisional GR*
*Ghisonaccia - Ajaccio*
*crosses the GR20.*

**6:00**

Continue down again through beech and pine trees, with occasional glimpse of the Taravu villages. After crossing several small streams the footpath joins a track; follow this for 2 kilometres to A Ruja, 1,240 metres, then close to a large level area into the beautiful Cerutti forest of Laricio, or Corsican pines. Cross the Benedetta stream to a small plateau at Faetalla, 1,079 metres. After crossing the Biancone stream the footpath continues to Ciuffali, and the village of Cozzano comes into view. Quite soon you cross a path coming from the GR20, and after 10 minutes' descent reaches the Ponte di Mezzanu bridge on the northeastern edge of Cozzano village.

**COZZANO**
⌂ ♆ ⚒
*727m*
**Giovicacce**
*Old mill at Giovicacce*
*restored by Nature Park.*

The footpath to Sampolo leaves from the southern edge of Cozzano. A short descent leads to Ponte di u Pinu, then rapidly to the little hamlet of a Parata. Continue gently up to Sampolo, 800 metres, through the village, and take the footpath from the southern edge down through hairpin bends to the Barbalatu stream,

close to the hamlet of Giovicacce, where the Nature Park has restored a flour mill. To pick up the path to Tasso take the D28 road northwest for about 500 metres. The path turns off west through Saparelle, then through a beautiful chestnut wood before climbing to Tasso, cutting across the D128 twice on the way.

From the middle of the village take a footpath to Pineto, then on to the southwest through a large chestnut wood close to Arja Petraja. The next stretch is across an easy slope, crossing the Filetta and Cadutu streams. A gentle climb leads to the 955 metres altitude marker at Quarciu Pianu. Turn south at the junction with the path to Bocca di Lera. From there the path drops swiftly down to the middle of Guitera.

**Alternative route** from Cozzano to Guitera-les-Bains via Zicavo. Take the footpath from near the centre of Cozzano village, steeply up through woods - first chestnuts, then beeches - to the altitude marker at 1,017 metres. The climb becomes gentler, reaching a large plateau by the Pinettu sheep-pen, with a view over Porto Pollo and the Col de Verde, and the path continues across the flank to Focicchia, 1,150 metres. After crossing two small streams and a path running back to join the GR20 at Bocca di l'Agnone, or Manoga, the descent becomes steep, down through woods mainly of chestnuts which are probably the oldest in the area. The path reaches Zicavo near the San Roccu chapel to the north of the villge.

To pick up the footpath to Les Bains de Guitera, go right through Zicavo village to the southern edge, near the San Bastianu chapel. Cross the Grimaldu bridge, then after a slight rise the path briefly drops down quite steeply, calling for some caution. Next, cross the Cavatella stream by a fixed footbridge, then climb up a long slope through tall maquis, and cross a movable footbridge into the village of Bains de Guitera, at 450 metres. Take the footpath

## Timeline (left margin)

2:20

**TASSO**
🏠 ✕ ☆
830m

2:10

**GUITERA-LES- BAINS**
🏠 ✕ ☆ ⚖
621m
Thermal springs.

**COZZANO**
🏠 ☆ ⚖
727m

2:15

**ZICAVO**
Ⓗ 🏠 ✕ ☆ ⚖
725m
Leisure facilities: tennis, swimming, canoeing/kayak in April - May.

2:15

from the middle of the village, to Calcinaju, and then across the Camproni stream. This comes out on the D28 road beside the charcuterie co-operative, and the hostel is 300 metres farther on towards the village of Guitera-Les-Bains.

**Guitera-les-Bains**

3:30

Take the footpath which leaves near the village wash-house, heading steadily up through the maquis, passing first the 853 metres altitude marker at Scialmaccia, then close to Punta di Bozzi, 1,088 metres. From a small clearing the villages of Cozzano and Zicavo are still visible, and you soon reach the Bocca di Lera, 1,048 metres, a magnificent broad plateau, partly wooded and criss-crossed by numerous footpaths. Continue heading west for the walk down to Frasseto, passing near the Ballatoju spring, and then through an oak wood to Cruciatu di Tuacara, 952 metres. Note also in damp areas the many sweet-chestnut plantations. The path drops gently down southwestwards, with views of Punta Usciolu and Punta di Forca d'Olmu, and after passing through Braccia and Vadigonu reaches the north of Frasseto, joining a motor road for about 600 metres into the middle of the village. To pick up the footpath again take the Campo road, and 150 metres beyond the bridge over the river Chiova, turn off right. The path runs up westwards through tall maquis, and then through a large chestnut wood, passing a tomb near the footpath shortly before reaching the village of Quasquara.

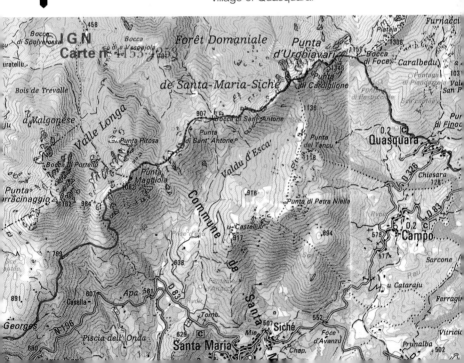

# T
## QUASQUARA

⌂ ♨

**721m**
*Swimming pool.*

6:00

The footpath sets off above the village, climbing rapidly to Bocca di Foce, 1,150 metres, across the Arena plateau, and then southwest along the ridge overlooking the Gulf of Ajaccio. Next it runs through Bocca di Sant'Antone, on to Punta Maggiola and Punta di a Crena, then up through oak woods to Col Saint-Georges.

## COL SAINT GEORGES

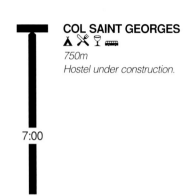

*750m*
*Hostel under construction.*

7:00

This route is given for general information, while the hostel at Col Saint-Georges is still under construction. Take the footpath close to the auberge at the Col. After a short climb the path reaches a long shoulder near the 890 metres altitude marker, then continues along the contour line to Bocca di Travu, 832 metres. After an easy descent to the D55, the path crosses the road at Bocca d'Aja di Bastiano, 638 metres, a few hundred metres from the village of Bisinao and follows the bank of the Campestra stream. On reaching the D255, turn left along the road for about 2 kilometres to reach Pietrosella.

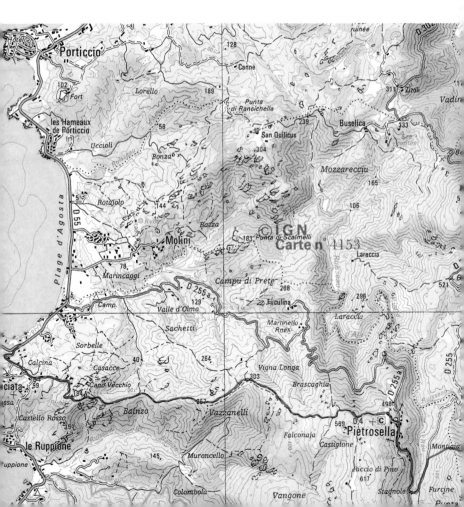

© I G N
Carte n° 4153

**Pietrosella**

**AJACCIO**
Ⓗ ✕ ♈ ⚖ 🎫

The path starts again beside the village church, and after a short climb goes steadily down a fairly long slope to Cruciata. From here there are coaches to Ajaccio town centre several times a day.

# WALK 5

This footpath is practicable at all times of year, and presents no real problems, even for inexperienced walkers; it is recommended for family outings. The route is arrowed and waymarked in orange. It enables walkers to explore a magnificent area of moderate altitude and appreciate its traditions: L'Alta Rocca, the Ospedale forest and its lake, the Bavella pinnacles, the Coscione plateau are just a few of the area's natural treasures.

**PORTO VECCHIO**

4:30

The footpath itself starts at `Alzu di Gallina', 7 kilometres from Porto Vecchio. To reach it, take the D159 road from the crossroads at Quatre Chemins outside Porto Vecchio towards Muratellu, then fork right towards Nota. The route is waymarked. Follow the road to the bridge over the River Bala, cross the river and take the first right turn after the bridge. From Alzu di Gallina the footpath heads northwest across a broad plateau covered in maquis, from where the village of l'Ospedale is visible ahead. The track then climbs steadily up and into a wood of maritime pines. Continue through the wood for about 1 hour 30 minutes, crossing the RF11 forest track four times, then bear west towards a plateau from which the first house in l'Ospedale can be seen. The footpath leads through l'Ospedale, bears left 200 metres beyond the last house, crosses a small stream, and then goes up through the woods to the plateau of Cartalavone, 1,020 metres.

**CARTALAVONU**

*1,020m*

5:00

The footpath heads northnorthwest along a track for about 200 metres, then climbs rapidly up above the hamlet, with views over the Gulf of Ponte Vecchio. After passing the first col the path continues steadily to Foce Alta, 1,171 metres, overlooking the Ospedale lake, and on towards the Col de Mela, 1,068 metres. At the foot of the slope, bear right to a mass of granite rocks where the view is magnificent: on the extreme left the Gulf of Valincu, then the Alta Rocca villages. Also visible are the peaks of Alcudina and Bavella, and part of the Coscione plateau. The footpath continues to the left, runs briefly beside a fence, then into the woods once more. After twenty minutes' gentle and easy descent, you come out of the woods into the tall maquis. The path winds through arbutus and heather, with the village

111

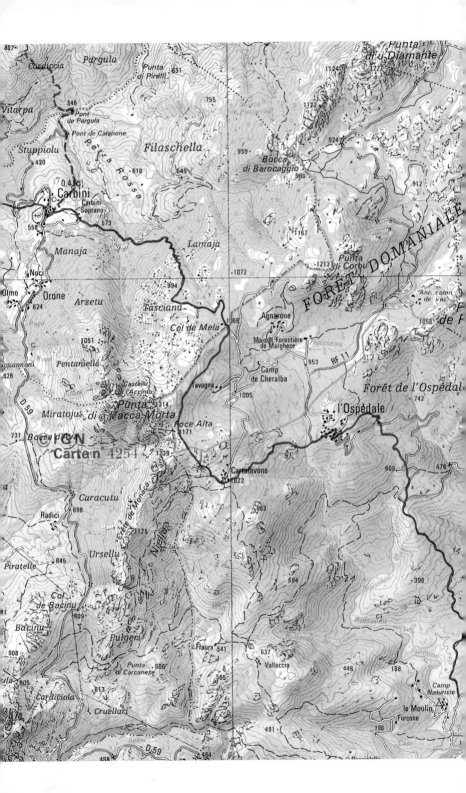

# FLORA OF CORSICA

### `U Castagnu': the Sweet Chestnut

The sweet chestnut woods of Evisa, Cristinacce and Marignana, an essential element of traditional culture, form an enormous and entirely man-made plantation. The chestnuts were used in great quantity for food. The blossom appears in July and long yellowish catkins cover the trees until they fall to the ground, followed in November by the ripe chestnuts and their husks. The Corsicans also use the chestnut wood, which is strong and impervious to rot, for fencing, beams and roof-timbers, furniture, etc. Chestnuts are a long-lived species and the older trees have witnessed several centuries of Corsican history.

### `L'Albitru': the Arbutus

Above the Pianu Maio ridge the footpath winds across a small plateau among beautiful arbutus groves. This small tree, characteristic of the maquis, grows to a height of 7 metres. Its evergreen leaves, dark on their upper surface, shine in the sun. The arbutus flowers between December and February, at the same time bearing the fruit from the previous year's flowers; the fruit can be used to make an excellent jelly.

### `U Ghjineparu': Juniper

Remarkable century-old junipers cover the Capu San Petru ridge, growing to the west beyond the maritime pines. The juniper tree with its twisted trunk and branches bears pea-sized blue-black berries, and its sharply pointed leaves are barely 1cm long. Juniper wood was much sought after by traditional craftsmen for the utensils needed for making `brocciu' cheeses, milking the ewes, etc.

### `A scopa': Heather

Great swathes of honey-scented white flowers appear on the clumps of white heather in the maquis from March onwards; the bushy plants are usually between 1 and 2 metres in height, but may reach 5 metres. Needing little light, heather often grows in woods, particularly under maritime pines and sweet chestnuts. The branches can be used as simple brooms, and the woody stems bundled into faggots to heat the ovens for baking bread, while the roots are used to make fine `briar' pipes.

### `U Laricciu': the Laricio, or Corsican Pine

Between the altitudes of 1,000 metres and 1,800 metres, this tree is king of the Corsican forest. Nowhere else does it reach the same height or quality. Individual specimens may be 50 metres high, with a diameter of more than 2 metres. Valued from the days of antiquity for making ships' masts, decimated by careless cutting since 1860, its qualities of fine grain, resistance to weathering and inherent stength, and ease of working make its timber outstandingly useful for construction and for furniture, for which it deserves to be better known and appreciated.

### `A Morta': Myrtle

A sweet-scented bush with deep green leaves, covered in white flowers in June, myrtle grows particularly well on slopes near the sea. Its stems were used in earlier times to weave lobster pots and baskets, and it leaves for tanning hides. It was also valued in the kitchen for flavouring charcuterie and wine. Nowadays myrtle is mostly prized for its berries, which are dried and infused in brandy to make a delicious liqueur.

of Carbini and its handsome bell-tower visible below. Shortly after reaching a chestnut wood, you cross a track to reach Carbini. The footpath continues from in front of the church, heading west, and after long flat stretch crosses the D59 before ploughing through the maquis again and then a large oak-wood. It runs for a time between two boundary walls, crosses the River Fiumicicoli, and then begins the climb towards Levie. Leaving the walls and their surrounding oak trees, the track becomes broader, and the slope steeper. A little farther on you come to small fields planted with olive trees, and pass an abandoned olive-press. A long shoulder of shady hillside offers a good resting place. You then have only to cross three small streams, and before long reach the first houses of Levie.

The footpath starts again near the church, passes a fountain at the edge of the village, and climbs up through oak woods for twenty minutes to a road at 770 metres, with a view over the villages of Serra and Sorbollano. Follow this road to the northeast, towards Capula, and then a track winding between large granite blocks. A little farther on, you reach the Saint Laurent chapel, near which is a natural shelter hollowed out of a granite rock. Continue down the gently sloping path through an oak wood to a junction, where you turn right towards Zonza, then very shortly north again, down and across the Pian di Santu stream. The path climbs gently up to Zonza between walls, approaching the village from the south.

## LEVIE

610m
Archaeological sites, centre and museum; Leisure centre: horse riding, tennis, swimming.

**Detour,**
## BAVELLA

3:00

1,218m
Rock climbing; designated site.
The Hostel at the Bavella summer village, on the GR20, can be reached by following the D268 road northeastwards.

**ZONZA**

777m
Park Information Centre;
racecourse.

1:50

From the roundabout in the middle of Zonza take the D420 road to Quenza. After 1 kilometre, at a sign to Funtanaccia, turn left off the road onto a footpath, and almost immediately afterwards take a track to the right, through a shady area of chestnut trees. Then follow a footpath down across a stream and then a ravine to reach a cleared hollow, and the Criviscia stream. After crossing the stream follow the path through a plantation of maritime pines, bear promptly to the left, along a wall, and then into wood of ilex. After 30 minutes this brings you to a small stream, running beside it for 200 metres, then turning away to the left and climbing up through the wood and back to the D420. Turn left along the road for 600 metres to reach the village of Quenza.

**QUENZA**

820m
11th century chapel; church
a designated site;
swimming, horse riding,
climbing (at Bavella).

1:30

From the square in front of the church, take the road up to the Coscione plateau. After about 200 metres turn left onto a footpath to the Codi stream where swimming is possible. Cross the stream by the footbridge and follow the track up through the oak wood to meet the road again at Buri. Follow it left, for 100 metres, then turn right on to the footpath leading through thick shady brushwood. The slope becomes steep and you reach a bare height with views over Quenza and Zonza. A little farther on the footpath rejoins the track to the Jallicu plateau.

**JALLICU**

1,107m

3:30

From Jallicu take the footpath to the right of the road; for 15 minutes it follows the contour line, then descends through the maquis of heather, arbutus, and maritime pines towards the Lavu Donacu sheep-pens. Pass old chestnut mill beside the river, cross the stream, and climb up again, southwestwards, towards the sheep-pens. The path continues through a semi-desert area with thorn-bushes and heather to Bocca d'Arja Petrosa. The vast plateau here is still used to rear sheep, cattle and pigs, and 4 or 5 shepherds live up here from June to October. In the distance the mountain massifs of Bavella and Alcudina are visible. Continuing southwards the path follows the contour line and after crossing the Arja La Foce col at 1,040 metres bears away right.

The view opens up over the villages of Serra di Scopamène and Sorbollano, and the track descends gently down to Bocca di Pardisu at 969 metres. Soon you come out onto a motor track leading to the campsite and then the village of Serra.

## SERRA-DI-SCOPAMÈNE
△ 人 ✕ 𝖸 ♨

*850m*
*Restored mill; horse riding, tennis.*

**6:00**

From the middle of Serra take the lane running below the main street, and pass the last houses of the village before turning into the chestnut wood. From there you can see the mill restored by the Regional Park, now a meeting hall. The path turns right at the Park sign, soon reaching a small ilex wood, then passes close to the old ruined hamlet of Mamma, and comes out onto the D20. Follow the road to the right for about 500 metres, to Campu; then take the footpath, left, down through a meadow and across a stream, which you follow for about 20 minutes down to the River Rizzanese. Cross the river and climb up through a wood of oaks and arbutus, then into a chestnut wood, past the Latachi spring, to reach an open area with a view over Serra and Sorbollano, the Bavella peaks, and the summit of Alducina. The path continues steadily up to the Col de Tarava, 720 metres, with a panoramic view over the Alta Rocca and villages, carries on to the Tarava spring, then turns left, across some scree and then a stream, to run gently along the contour line under a magnificent wood of ilex. Passing two stretches of rock, you join a motor track leading into the village of Altagene. From there you continue along the path, which runs between walls to the hamlet of Sant'Andrea di Talla, and very quickly reaches the village of Sainte-Lucie-de-Tallano.

## SAINTE-LUCIE-DE-TALLANO
⌂ 人 ✕ ♨

*450m*
*15th century convent and tower; 12th century Norman chapel in church of St. John Baptist on the path to Loreto-di-Talla.*

**2:00**

From the village square take the lane to the hamlet of Poggio, where the footpath turns left off the D20 road after a slight descent, and follows the contour line north and then west to the church of St. John the Baptist. Continue down through the oak wood to the River Rizzanese, and along the bank for 400 metres, to cross it by the Pimbato bridge. The footpath continues to the right, following a track for about 100 metres, plunges into the oak trees again, then climbs steadily between walls to the village of Loreto di Tallano.

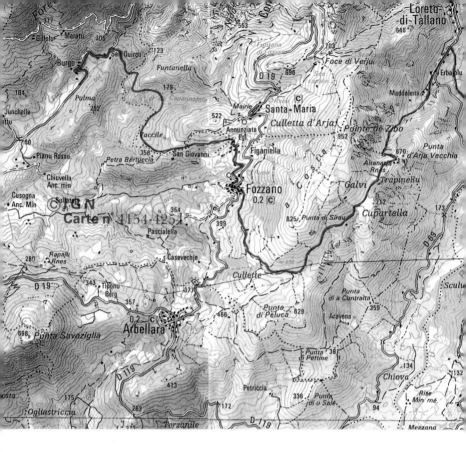

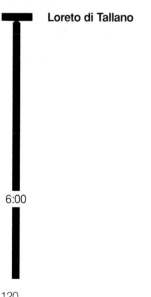

## Loreto di Tallano

**6:00**

From Loreto the footpath heads southsouthwest along a track which climbs up through the valley to reach the ruins of Altanaria in about 1 hour 15 minutes. It continues along the ridge at about 700 metres, with the Bavella pinnacles visible in the distance, also the Alcudina massif and the villages of Serra di Scopamena, Sorbollano, Cargiaca, Loreto and Santa Lucia di Talla, as well as the plain of the Rizzanese to the south. The path carries on along the contour line, past the Calvi and Pinvanaccia ravines, then begins to descend, curving around to the right until it bears northnorthwest, and continues to Fozzano, arriving there after about 3 hours' walking from Loreto. From Fozzano you have 2 options: 1. Head north on the D19 tarmac road for about 600 metres, to rejoin the main route at Figaniella. 2. To reach the Baraci plain, take the path west from the village centre, past the Colomba tomb, and through the oak trees

to join the track suitable for vehicles, at Sullataja, leading to the Filetta bridge which is 3 kilometres by road from the beach at Baraci, and 5 kilometres by road from Propriano.

**PROPRIANO**

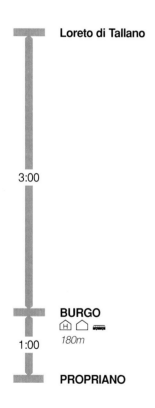

**Loreto di Tallano**

**Alternative route** Take a tarmac lane above the church, then climb rapidly through ilex and over a saddle, bear left, and continue southwest along the valley to reach the Col de Verju at 703 metres, 2 hours' walking from Loreto - with a fine view over the gulf of Valincu. The track goes through the hamlet and down towards Santa Maria; 15 minutes' walk will bring you into the village, past the twelfth-century church and on to Figaniello. The path runs between the houses, across a stream, and along the contour line, with a view over the villages of Fozzano and Arbellara - which are worth a visit - to a shoulder overlooking the gulf of Valincu. Curving round in a wide bend to the right, northwest, it drops steadily down through the oak woods, and crosses the Caparnajola steam, then the River Baaci, near an old mill. The path runs up the right bank of the river, then bears left and climbs up through the maquis to Burgo.

3:00

**BURGO**
Ⓗ ⌂ 🚌
*180m*

From Burgo the D557 motor road leads to Propriano, 7 kilometres away.

1:00

**PROPRIANO**

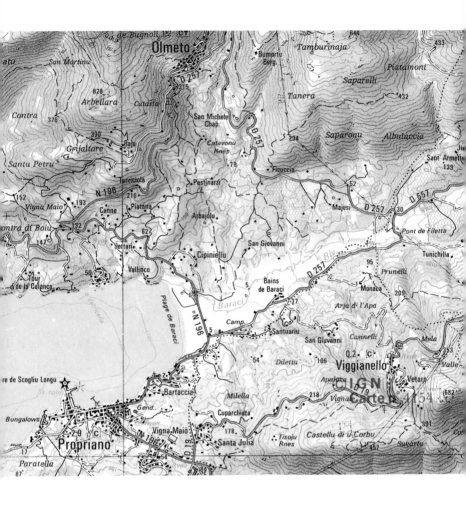

# ACCOMMODATION GUIDE

The many different kinds of accommodation in France are explained in the introduction. Here we include a selection of hotels and other addresses, which is by no means exhaustive – the hotels listed are usually in the one-star or two-star categories. We have given full postal addresses where available so bookings can be made.

There has been an explosive growth in bed and breakfast facilities (chambres d'hôte) in the past few years, and staying in these private homes can be especially interesting and rewarding. Local shops and the town hall (mairie) can usually direct you to one.

**Abbazia**
⌂
*Mme Susini*
☎ *95.56.02.29*

**Alando**
*20250 Corte*
⌂
*Mr Défendini*
☎ *95.48.66.72*

**Ajaccio**
*20000 Corse*
⌂ *Bella Vista*
*Boulevard Sylvestre-Marcaggi*
*Mr Jean Baptiste Giovannelli*
☎ *95.21.07.97*
⌂ *Creste e Mare*
*Route des Sanguinaires*
*Mr Massei*
☎ *95.21.66.63*
⌂ *Imperial*
*6 Boulevard Albert 1er*
*Mme Fieschi*
☎ *95.21.50.62*
⌂ *Napoléon*
*4 rue Lorenzo Véro*
*Mr Fratani*
☎ *95.21.30.01*
⌂ *San Carlu*
*8 Boulevard D. Casanova*
*Mr Antonioli*
☎ *95.21.13.84*

**Albertacce**
*20224 Calacuccia*
⌂
*Mr Albertini*
☎ *95.48.05.60*

**Bavella**
⌂ *Bavella*
*Mr Grimaldi*

☎ *95.57.43.87*

**Bonifatu**
*20214 Calenzana*
⌂ *de la Foret*
☎ *95.65.09.98*
*or 95.62.70.14*

**Burgo**
⌂ *"U Fracintu"*
*Mr J. Angelini*
☎ *95.76.15.05*
*or 95.20.53.14*

**Calacuccia**
⌂ *des touristes*
☎ *95.48.00.04*
⌂ *de la Scala*
☎ *95.48.05.60*

**Calenzana**
*20214 Calenzana*
⌂
☎ *95.62.70.08*

**Cartalavonu**
⌂
*Mr Monti*
☎ *95.70.00.39*

**Casanova**
*20250 Corte*
⌂
*Mr Perfettini*
☎ *95.47.03.17*

**Catastaghju**
⌂
*Mr Bartoli*
☎ *95.56.70.53*
*or 95.56.73.34*

**Castellare**

⌂
*Mr Giudicelli*
☎ *95.48.66.72*

**Col Saint Georges**
⌂
*Mme Renucci*
☎ *95.15.70.06*

**Corter**
⌂
☎ *95.46.27.44*

**Cozzano**
*20148 Cozzano*
⌂
*Mr Pantalacci*
☎ *95.24.41.59*

**Curzu**
*20147 Portinello*
⌂
*Mr Colonna Francois*
☎ *95.27.31.70*

**Galéria**
*20245 Galéria*
⌂
*Mr Rossi*
☎ *95.62.00.21*
*or 95.62.00.46*

**Ghjallicu**
⌂
*Mr Milanini*
☎ *95.78.63.21*
⌂
☎ *95.78.62.53*

**Girolata**
*20147 Partinello*
⌂
☎ *95.26.10.98*

⌂
*Mr Luciani*
☎ *95. 20.16.98*

**Guagno**
⌂
☎ *95.28.31.24*

**Guitéra**
*20153 Guitéra*
⌂
*Mr Lanfanchi*
☎ *95.24.42.54*

**Marignana**
⌂
*Mr P. Ceccaldi*
☎ *95.26.21.21*

**Noceta**
*20219 Vivario*
⌂
☎ *95.44.00.02*
⌂
☎ *95.44.03.75*

**Ota**
⌂
☎ *95.26.10.05*
⌂
*Mr Ceccaldi*
☎ *95.26.12.92*

**Pianello**
*20250 Corte*
⌂
*Mr Z. Kurt*

☎ *95.44.21.39*

**Poggio de Venaco**
⌂
*Mr Giorgetti*
☎ *95.47.02.19*
*or 95.47.03.00*

**Renno**
⌂
☎ *95.26.65.35*

**Révinda** ?
⌂
☎ *95.21.56.54*

**Santa Lucia di Tallano**
⌂
*Mme Leandri*
☎ *95.78.80.82*

**Sermano**
*20250 Corte*
⌂
*Mr Mariani*
☎ *95.48.66.67*
*or 95.48.67.97*

**Serra di Fiumborbu**
⌂
*Mr Guidicelli*
☎ *95.56.72.54*

**Serriera**
*20147 Partinello*
⌂
*Mr Corbani*

☎ *95.26.10.67*

**Soccia**
⌂ *"U Paese"*
☎ *95.28.31.92*

**Tasso**
*20132 Zicavo*
⌂
☎ *95.24.52.01*

**Tuarelli**
*20245 Galeria*
⌂
*Mr Mariani*
☎ *95.62.01.75*

**Vivario**
⌂
☎ *95.47.00.11*

**Zicavo**
⌂
☎ *95.24.43.54*
⌂
☎ *95.24.40.05*
⌂
☎ *95.24.40.06*
*or 95.24.43.11*

**Zonza**
⌂ *Le mouflon d'or*
☎ *95.78.67.34*
⌂
☎ *95.78.67.79*
*or 95.78.67.71*
*or 95.78.66.04*

# INDEX

Details of bus/train connections have been provided wherever it was possible. We suggest you refer also to the map inside the front cover.